THE BOOK LOVER'S GUIDE TO OXFORD

THE BOOK LOVER'S GUIDE TO OXFORD

ANGELA YOUNGMAN

WHITE OWL
AN IMPRINT OF PEN & SWORD BOOKS LTD.
YORKSHIRE – PHILADELPHIA

First published in Great Britain in 2026
White Owl
An imprint of
Pen & Sword Books Ltd
Yorkshire – Philadelphia

ISBN 978 1 03611 814 3

A CIP catalogue record for this book is available from the British Library.

Printed and bound in India by Replika Press Pvt. Ltd.
Design: SJmagic DESIGN SERVICES, India.

The Publisher's authorised representative in the EU for product safety is Authorised Rep Compliance Ltd., Ground Floor, 71 Lower Baggot Street, Dublin D02 P593, Ireland.
www.arccompliance.com

For a complete list of Pen & Sword titles please contact

PEN & SWORD BOOKS LIMITED
George House, Beevor Street, Off Pontefract Road, Hoyle Mill, Barnsley, South Yorkshire, England, S71 1HN.
E-mail: enquiries@pen-and-sword.co.uk
Website: www.pen-and-sword.co.uk

or

PEN AND SWORD BOOKS
1950 Lawrence Road, Havertown, PA 19083, USA
E-mail: uspen-and-sword@casematepublishers.com
Website: www.penandswordbooks.com

FSC
www.fsc.org
MIX
Paper | Supporting responsible forestry
FSC™ C016779

CONTENTS

PART 1: OXFORD AND LITERATURE............8
THE MURDER CAPITAL OF THE UK..........10
OXFORD UNIVERSITY..............................12
FESTIVALS 14
ALICE'S DAY..14
CHIPPING NORTON LITERARY FESTIVAL...15
OXCON 15
OXFORD LITERARY FESTIVAL..............15
PHOENIX FEST.......................................16
ST HILDA'S COLLEGE CRIME FICTION WEEKEND 16

GUIDED TOURS 16

LITERARY ASSOCIATIONS BY AUTHOR....16
BRIAN ALDISS...16
KINGSLEY AMIS......................................17
MATTHEW ARNOLD 17
JANE AUSTEN...17
SIR HENRY MAXIMILIAN BEERBOHM....18
HILAIRE BELLOC.....................................19
ALAN BENNETT 19
SIR JOHN BETJEMAN 19
VERA BRITTAIN......................................20
JOHN BUCHAN.......................................20
LEWIS CARROLL.....................................21
GEOFFREY CHAUCER............................22
G.K. CHESTERTON.................................23
AGATHA CHRISTIE.................................23
WINSTON CHURCHILL..........................24
SUSAN COOPER 24
CRESSIDA COWELL 25
EDMUND CRISPIN..................................26
ROALD DAHL..26
CECIL DAY-LEWIS..................................26
THOMAS DE QUINCEY..........................27
COLIN DEXTER.......................................27
CHARLES DICKENS JR 29
JOHN DONNE...30
T.S. ELIOT...30
JAMES GORDON FARRELL 30
HELEN FIELDING...................................31
WILLIAM FIENNES.................................31
IAN FLEMING 31
JOHN FOWLES 31
ANTONIA FRASER 31
JOHN GALSWORTHY.............................32
ALAN GARNER 32
WILLIAM GOLDING 32
KENNETH GRAHAME 32
ROBERT GRAVES 33
GRAHAM GREENE 34
ROGER LANCELYN GREEN....................34
MARK HADDON 35
THOMAS HARDY....................................35
DEBORAH HARKNESS 35
HAZEL HOLT...36
GERARD MANLEY HOPKINS.................36
A.E. HOUSMAN 37
THOMAS HUGHES.................................37
MICHAEL INNES 37
P.D. JAMES 38
SAMUEL JOHNSON 38
ANDREW LANG......................................39
PHILIP LARKIN 40
T.E. LAWRENCE......................................40
JOHN LE CARRÉ......................................41
C.S. LEWIS 42
PENELOPE LIVELY..................................43
THOMAS LOVELL BEDDOES................44
COMPTON MACKENZIE 44
ROSE MACULAY......................................44
FAITH MARTIN 44
GUILLERMO MARTINEZ.......................45
JOHN MASEFIELD..................................45
JOHN MASTERMAN...............................45
VAL MCDERMID 46
THE MITFORD SISTERS........................46
GEOFFREY OF MONMOUTH 47
SIR THOMAS MORE 47
WILLIAM MORRIS..................................48
IAN MORSON 48
IRIS MURDOCH......................................49
V.S. NAIPAUL 49
S.J. PARRIS..50
WALTER PATER 50
PHILIP PULLMAN 50

BARBARA PYM 52
SIR ARTHUR QUILLER-COUCH .. 52
J.K. ROWLING 52
JOHN RUSKIN 54
SIEGFRIED SASSOON 55
DOROTHY L. SAYERS 55
VIKRAM SETH 56
DR SEUSS 56
WILLIAM SHAKESPEARE 56
PERCY BYSSHE SHELLEY 57
SIR PHILIP SIDNEY 58
ROBERT SOUTHEY 58
STEPHEN SPENDER 58
VERONICA STALLWOOD 58
ROSEMARY SUTCLIFF 59
JONATHAN SWIFT 59
ALGERNON SWINBURNE 59
ANN SWINFEN 59
DYLAN THOMAS 60
CHARLES TODD 60
J.R.R. TOLKIEN 60
SIMON TOLKIEN 62
JOANNA TROLLOPE 63
EVELYN WAUGH 63
JOHN AND CHARLES WESLEY 63
OSCAR WILDE 64
CHARLES WILLIAMS 64

PART 2: KEY LOCATIONS 65
OXFORD CITY CENTRE 65
ADDISON'S WALK 65
ALICE'S SHOP 65
ASHMOLEAN MUSEUM 67
BLACKWELL'S BOOKSHOP 68
BODLEIAN LIBRARY 69
BRASENOSE LANE 70
BREWER STREET 70
BRIDGE OF SIGHS 71
BROAD STREET 72
BROWN'S CAFÉ 73
CARFAX 74
DIVINITY SCHOOL 75
EASTGATE HOTEL 76
FOLLY BRIDGE 76
HISTORY OF SCIENCE MUSEUM .77
HOLYWELL MILL 77
LAMB & FLAG PUB 78
MAGDALEN BRIDGE BOATHOUSE 79
MAGPIE LANE 81
MATHEMATICAL INSTITUTE 81
MERTON STREET 82
MUSEUM OF OXFORD 83
NO. 3 CORNMARKET 84
OLD PARSONAGE HOTEL 84
OSNEY ABBEY 86
OXFORD BOTANIC GARDEN 86
OXFORD CANAL 88
OXFORD CASTLE 88
OXFORD RAILWAY STATION 90
OXFORD UNION 90
OXFORD UNIVERSITY MUSEUM OF NATURAL HISTORY 91
OXFORD UNIVERSITY PRESS MUSEUM 92
PITT RIVERS MUSEUM 94
PORT MEADOW 94
RADCLIFFE CAMERA 95
RANDOLPH HOTEL 97
RIVER CHERWELL 98
RIVER ISIS 99
SHELDONIAN THEATRE 100
ST ALDATE'S POLICE STATION .. 101
ST ALDATE'S STREET 102
ST ALOYSIUS CHURCH 103
ST MARY MAGDALENE CHURCH 103
ST MARY THE VIRGIN CHURCH 103
ST MARY'S PASSAGE 104
THE COVERED MARKET 104
THE EAGLE AND CHILD PUB 105
THE STORY MUSEUM 107
TURF TAVERN 108
WESLEY MEMORIAL CHURCH .. 109
WHITE HORSE PUB 109

OXFORD COLLEGES 110
ALL SOULS COLLEGE 110
BALLIOL COLLEGE 111
BRASENOSE COLLEGE 112
CHRIST CHURCH 113
CHRIST CHURCH CATHEDRAL 115
CHRIST CHURCH GARDENS 117
CHRIST CHURCH MEADOW 117
CLARENDON QUAD 118
DEANERY, CHRIST CHURCH 119
CORPUS CHRISTI COLLEGE 119
EXETER COLLEGE 121
HERTFORD COLLEGE 122
JESUS COLLEGE 123
KEBLE COLLEGE 124
LADY MARGARET HALL 125
LINCOLN COLLEGE 127
MAGDALEN COLLEGE 128
MERTON COLLEGE 130
NEW COLLEGE 131
ORIEL COLLEGE 132
PEMBROKE COLLEGE 133
RUSKIN SCHOOL OF ART 134
SOMERVILLE COLLEGE 135
ST ANNE'S COLLEGE 136
ST CROSS COLLEGE 137
ST HILDA'S COLLEGE 137
ST HUGH'S COLLEGE 139
ST JOHN'S COLLEGE 139
THE QUEEN'S COLLEGE 140
TRINITY COLLEGE 142
UNIVERSITY COLLEGE 143
WADHAM COLLEGE 144
WORCESTER COLLEGE 145

OUTER OXFORD 147
AMPLEFORTH ARMS PUB 147
BOARS HILL 147
C.S. LEWIS NATURE RESERVE 148
DRAGON SCHOOL 149
THE HARCOURT ARMS PUB 150
HEADINGTON 151
HOLY TRINITY CHURCH 152
HOLYWELL CEMETARY 153
JERICHO 154
JUDE THE OBSCURE PUB 154
NORTHMOOR ROAD 155
NORTH OXFORD 156
OLD BOOKBINDERS ALE HOUSE 156
10 OLD HIGH STREET 157
2 POLSTEAD ROAD 158
SANDFIELD ROAD 159
ST ANDREW'S CHURCH 160
ST CROSS CHURCH 160
SUMMERTOWN 161
THE KILNS 162
THE TROUT INN 163
THE VICTORIA ARMS PUB 165
WOLVERCOTE 166
WOLVERCOTE CEMETERY 166

OXFORDSHIRE 167
ASTHALL MANOR 167
BINSEY: CHURCH OF ST MARGARET OF ANTIOCH 169
BLENHEIM PALACE 170
BLEWBURY 173
CHARLBURY 174
EWELME: ST MARY THE VIRGIN 174
FINSTOCK 175
FLEECE PUB, WITNEY 176
FOUR SHIRE STONE 176
GODSTOW 177
ISLIP 178
KELMSCOTT MANOR 178
NETTLEBED 180
ROLLRIGHT STONES 180
SOUTH LEIGH 182
SWINBROOK: ST MARY'S CHURCH 182
SWINBROOK: THE SWAN INN 183
UFFINGTON 184
WALLINGFORD 185
WANTAGE 186
WINTERBROOK 187
WOODSTOCK 189

1

OXFORD AND LITERATURE

Best known for its links with J.R.R. Tolkien, C.S. Lewis, *Alice in Wonderland*, Harry Potter and Inspector Morse, Oxford abounds with literary associations covering most styles of writing, ranging from the works of Jane Austen to John Betjeman, Agatha Christie to Philip Pullman. As a historic university city, Oxford has attracted countless writers over the centuries, resulting in many authors having attended its various colleges. Numerous others, such as Ian Morson and S.J. Parrish have used it as a location or have lived in the area. The result is that Oxford and the surrounding areas are brimming with literary links, as well as literary festivals appealing to a wide range of tastes.

▼ ***The dreaming spires of Oxford.*** (Mick Crawley Geography .org. uk Wikimedia Commons)

Not surprisingly, Oxford is also a tourist destination, attracting over 23 million visitors each year. Visitors come from all over the world to visit Oxford and its collegiate 'dreaming spires'. The vast array of literary associations frequently leading to films and TV programmes like *Midsomer Murders* and *Inspector Morse* has added to the area's popularity, making it a must-see destination for countless visitors.

Oxford and its surrounds has produced more published authors per square mile than anywhere else in the world. It holds countless literary events every year, and is an area that has not only encouraged the development of writers through its university links but inspired yet more due to its special character. Over 500 novels have been identified as having links with Oxford and this number continues to increase as more and more authors use it as a location.

The first known fictional mention of Oxford occurs in Geoffrey Chaucer's *Canterbury Tales*. Responsible for popularising Middle English as an alternative to French and Latin, the *Tales* is a collection of stories written

▲ **Alice in Wonderland *at the Alice Day Festival.*** (© The Story Museum)

▲ ***Alice characters at the Alice Day festival.*** (© The Story Museum)

▲ ***The Clerk of Oxford from the Ellesmere Chaucer.***
(© Huntington Library, Wikimedia Commons)

between 1387 and 1400 as a way of entertaining a group of pilgrims travelling to Canterbury. Chaucer identifies one of the pilgrims as a Clerk of Oxford where he is studying logic, including the philosophy of Aristotle. A poor, hardworking student, he wears shabby, threadbare clothes and rides a lean horse. His story is about Grizelda, whose husband tests her loyalty with numerous cruel torments, including pretending to kill her child.

Oxfordshire has been involved in book printing since 1478 when Banbury was a centre for the printing of chapbooks (inexpensive booklets or pamphlets). The well known saying, 'red sky at night, shepherds delight' was first popularised in a Banbury chapbook.

THE MURDER CAPITAL OF THE UK

Oxford has long been nicknamed the 'murder capital of the UK'. It is a reputation first gained in medieval times. This was partly due to the fact that medieval students were young men aged between fourteen and twenty-one, living in an environment where they had weapons immediately to hand and easy access to alehouses and brothels. Their university teachers had little control over their behaviour. In 2023, a digital resource known as 'Medieval Murder Maps' added Oxford and York to its existing study of London's medieval murders, based on coroners' inquests. Oxford's homicide rate was up to five times higher than London or York. Oxford city records indicated that 75 per cent of killers were students, as were 72 per cent of victims. Clashes between students and townsfolk were all too common.

This Oxford crime link resurfaced in the twentieth century but this time focusing on fictional crimes. Oxford and the surrounding area has proved irresistible to crime writers. During the 'Golden Age of Crime Fiction' in

INSPECTOR
MORSE

▲ **Inspector Morse *TV series logo.***
(© Wikimedia Commons)

the 1920s and 1930s, the area featured in works by prominent writers such as Dorothy L. Sayers, Edmund Crispin and Michael Innes, while Agatha Christie made her home in Wallingford. This popularity has continued with countless crime novels are linked to the area, particularly those of Colin Dexter. And it is not just books that are involved, there are also the numerous film and TV spin-offs (such as *Morse*, *Lewis* and *Endeavour*, based on the original Inspector Morse books by Colin Dexter and *Midsomer Murders*, based on the *Inspector Barnaby* series by Caroline Graham) which often have several murders and crimes being committed in a single episode. Although Midsomer is a fictional county, many of the locations used in the filming are in Oxfordshire.

Writing in *Oxford Alumni*, author Andy Griffee commented that 'perhaps it is something to do with the inherent and long-standing tension between town and gown – a tension that can so easily erupt in violence on the page. Or is there some kind of challenging synthesis between the crime author's fiendishly puzzling plots and the first-rate brains of the academics they depict? There is certainly a visceral thrill for the reader who is briefly admitted into the hallowed spaces of the college's wood-panelled common rooms, hidden quads and high-vaulted dining halls.'

▼ ***Filming* Endeavour *in Merton Street, Oxford.*** (© Wikipedia Commons/Creative Commons)

OXFORD UNIVERSITY

Oxford University is the world's second oldest university, with only the University of Bologna being older. It is certainly the oldest university in the English speaking world, and has been in continuous existence for over 900 years. No one knows exactly when scholars and teachers first began congregating in Oxford, but it is believed that some form of teaching existed in 1096. In 1188, the historian Gerald of Wales gave a public reading in Oxford to fellow dons, while the first overseas student appeared in 1190 with the arrival of Emo of Friesland.

By 1201, a *Magister Scholarum Oxnie* had been appointed as head of all the students and dons, and in 1214 this title was changed to chancellor. By the early thirteenth century, students were living in houses and medieval halls of residence, with each hall being under the control of a master, marking the start of the college system used at the university today. The oldest colleges were established between 1249 and 1264, and were called University, Balliol and Merton. Within a century, Oxford University was winning praise from popes, governments and kings. King Edward III congratulated the university in 1355 for its contribution to learning, as well as the way in which

▸ ***Graduation day at the University of Oxford.***
(© Ninara, Wikimedia Commons/Creative Commons)

its graduates were providing services to the state.

Oxford University is different in structure to most other UK universities. It operates on a federal system involving thirty-six colleges, three societies and four private halls. Each college is totally independent and self-governing, possessing charters that have been granted by the monarch's privy council. The colleges are governed by a head of house elected by the college governing body composed of fellows, the majority of whom hold university posts.

Kellogg College, Reuben College and St Cross College do not have a royal charter and are known as societies. Each of these colleges is governed by a president, who has been appointed by the college council. The private halls were founded by Christian denominations and retain their religious character.

Students have to apply to individual colleges for entry, rather than the university. Thirty-two of the colleges and the permanent private halls accept undergraduates. All colleges, halls and societies accept postgraduate students as long as they have been admitted to the university.

Campion Hall, Green Templeton, Kellogg, Linacre, Reuben, St Antony, St Cross and Wolfson Colleges accept only postgraduate students. All Souls has only fellows and a warden.

All the colleges, societies and halls provide accommodation, social and sports facilities and libraries, and are responsible for undergraduate teaching and welfare.

The University of Oxford controls the content of courses, organises examinations, oversees theses and awards degrees, as well as providing resources such as central libraries, laboratories and museums. Most of the buildings linked specifically to the university, such as the Sheldonian Theatre and the Weston Library, which is now part of the Bodleian, are located in Broad Street.

FESTIVALS

There are several literary festivals held throughout Oxford and the surrounding area every year. These festivals offer the opportunity to have fun, participate in interactive themed activities, dress up and discover more about various characters and authors.

Alice's Day

Alice's Day is an annual festival held in early July, supported by Oxford City Council and The Story Museum. Events and activities are held throughout the city, but tend to be focused around key locations related to *Alice in Wonderland*. Alice and other characters can be found meandering around the city, especially in the central streets, The Covered Market, the Bodleian, the Ashmolean Museum, the Oxford

▼ ***Alice's Day festivities at The Story Museum.*** (© The Story Museum)

▲ ***Lively entertainment on Alice's Day.*** (© The Story Museum)

University Museum of Natural History, The Story Museum, Alice's Shop, Oxford Botanic Garden and the 'Treacle Well' in Binsey churchyard. Visitors can take part in *Alice in Wonderland* walking tours, picnics, workshops, street theatre, interactive storytelling, art installations and puppetry.

Chipping Norton Literary Festival

Held annually each April since 2012, the festival celebrates all aspects of reading and writing. Numerous writers and poets take part in talks, discussions and book signings at various venues around the town.

OxCon

Oxford's annual comic convention is usually held at the Examination Schools. Participants have included the Sixth Doctor Who, Colin Baker and David Prowse (Darth Vader). Some of the discussions and events reflect the area's literary and scientific links – for example, quantum physics and sci-fi.

Oxford Literary Festival

This annual event brings together authors and the public. The Bodleian Library is one of the festival's partners and many of the events take place there. During the week-long festival, marquees are set up all over the city acting as locations for book signings, author talks and a variety of literary activities. Participating authors have included Philip Pullman, Joanne Harris, Anthony Horowitz, Lauren Child, Penelope Lively and Ruby Wax.

Phoenix Fest
A children's comic festival linked to The Story Museum and the Oxford-based *The Phoenix* comic. Held once a year, it features appearances, talks and activities involving leading participants in children's comics, both writers and artists.

St Hilda's College Crime Fiction Weekend
St Hilda's College Crime Fiction Weekend was first held in 1994 and is now an annual event. It is held during August and features leading crime writers talking about their books and about crime writing in general. Among the writers who have taken part in the past are Elly Griffiths, Alexandra Benedict, Val McDermid, Mark Billingham and the Rev. Richard Coles. Themes vary, and have included 'Detecting the Gothic' and 'Dance to the Music of Crime'. A massive Blackwell's pop-up shop is located on site, and there are numerous author signings. Supported by the Crime Writers' Association, the weekend attracts participants from all over the world.

GUIDED TOURS

There are numerous guided tours of Oxford available on a regular basis, including many relating to literature. These include walking tours focusing on C.S. Lewis and J.R.R. Tolkien, *Alice in Wonderland*, Oscar Wilde, the Bodleian Old Library and literary Oxford. Such tours are provided by a variety of organisations including the University of Oxford and private tour operators. Generally they last between one and two hours, and include a variety of locations at which the guide provides background information and relevant stories.

LITERARY ASSOCIATIONS BY AUTHOR

These are by no means comprehensive, but include as many as possible that could be identified across all genres and historical time periods.

Brian Aldiss
Science fiction writer Brian Aldiss came to Oxford in 1947 after serving overseas during the Second World War. He took a job as an assistant at Sanders of Oxford, a bookshop on the High Street. After marrying his first wife Olive, he moved to 69 Victoria Street Summertown where he wrote his first science fiction novel. He eventually became literary editor of the *Oxford Mail*, and after marrying for the second

time, he and his wife Margaret moved to 39 St Andrew's Road, Old Headington. They lived there for the rest of their lives, having totally transformed the house to suit their requirements. Many of Aldiss's science fiction novels were written at that house. Brian Aldiss is buried at St Andrew's Church, Headington.

Locations: Headington, St Andrew's Church Headington

Kingsley Amis
In 1941 Kingsley Amis joined St John's College, reading English, and formed a close friendship with Philip Larkin and Edmund Crispin. His time at Oxford was affected by being called up in 1942 to serve in the Royal Corps of Signals. After being demobbed in 1945, he returned to Oxford to complete his degree. In 1947, he was awarded a first-class degree. After working for some years at the University College Swansea, his novel *Lucky Jim* was published and he subsequently devoted much of his time to writing. His semi-autobiographical novel *You Can't Do Both* includes references to studying in Oxford, while *Jake's Thing* features an Oxford don.

Location: St John's College

Matthew Arnold
The son of Thomas Arnold, headmaster of Rugby School, Matthew graduated from Balliol College in 1844. The following year, he was elected a fellow of Oriel College and in 1857 was elected Professor of Poetry, Oxford University. He was the first university professor to deliver lectures in English rather than Latin, and was a major Victorian poet and critic. Well-known works include *On Translating Homer*, *Culture and Anarchy* and *The Scholar Gipsy*.

Locations: Balliol College, Oriel College

Jane Austen
Jane Austen's family possessed long-standing links with Oxford. Her maternal grandfather, Thomas Leigh, was a fellow at All Souls College while Leigh's brother Theophilus was president of Balliol. It was during a visit to Theophilus that Cassandra Leigh first met Rev. George Austen, who studied at St John's, before gaining a fellowship at the college, teaching logic, Greek and natural philosophy. Cassandra's brother James was also studying at St John's. When Cassandra and George married, he had to resign his fellowship and sought a clerical position elsewhere. Since Cassandra Leigh was directly descended from Mary Bridgeman, sister of Sir Thomas White, her sons were able to claim 'founders' kin' fellowships at John's. In 1779, James Austen became a fellow of St John's, as did Henry in 1788.

Jane Austen lived in Oxford for a few months when she was seven years old. She and her sister Cassandra

▲ ***A is for Austen at the Bodleian.*** (Wikimedia Commons)

were attending a school run by Mrs Cawley, the widow of a former principal of Brasenose College who was also related to Jane's cousin Jane Cooper. Her brother James, a student at St John's, took the girls around the colleges. Jane later wrote that the experience 'gave me the vapours for two days afterwards', as it involved seeing 'dismal chapels, dusty libraries and greasy halls'. Despite this initial impression, she did in due course encourage her nephew Edward to take the same route saying, 'You must go to Oxford ... A little change of scene may be good for you.'

Many years later when she began writing novels, several of her male characters (all clergymen, such as Henry Tilney, Edmund Bertram, James Morland and Edward Ferrars), attended Oxford. In *Sense and Sensibility*, Edward Ferrars notes, 'I was ... entered at Oxford and have been properly idle ever since.'

In *Mansfield Park*, Jane wrote about Fanny's visit to Oxford saying, 'They entered Oxford, but she could take only a hasty glimpse of Edmund's college as they passed along.' The Weston Library, part of the Bodleian, houses special collections which includes works by Jane Austen.

Locations: All Souls College, Balliol College, Bodleian Library, St John's College

Sir Henry Maximilian Beerbohm

Essayist and caricaturist Max Beerbohm joined Merton College in 1890 and was secretary of its Myrmidon Club (a dining club exclusively for members of the college). Among his friends were Oscar Wilde and Aubrey Beardsley. He was an active participant in Oxford social life, while submitting numerous articles and caricatures for London publications. Beerbohm left Oxford without a degree. *Zuleika Dobson*, a burlesque study of Oxford life, was his only novel. Other works are included in numerous literary collections such as *The Works of Max Beerbohm* and *Caricatures of Twenty-Five Gentlemen.*

Locations: Magdalen Bridge Boathouse, Merton College, Randolph Hotel, River Cherwell

Hilaire Belloc

Of Anglo-French descent, Belloc attended Balliol College and was President of the Oxford Union. In 1893 he wrote:

> *Balliol made me, Balliol fed me,*
> *Whatever I had she gave me again;*
> *And the best of Balliol loved and*
> *led me,*
> *God be with you, Balliol men.*

While at Oxford, he and another student undertook the record-breaking feat of walking from Carfax Tower, Oxford, to Marble Arch, London in eleven and a half hours. At around fifty-five miles, this was more than double the distance of a marathon. He gained a first-class honours degree in history in 1895.

After marrying American Elodie Hogan, they settled initially in Oxford. Belloc became a naturalised British subject in 1902. He wrote historical biographies, travel books and comic verse for children, such as 'Jim, who ran away from his nurse, and was eaten by a lion', as well as religious poetry.

Locations: Balliol College, Carfax Tower

Alan Bennett

Actor, author and playwright Alan Bennett studied history at Exeter College. As a student he performed in the Oxford Revue. After graduating with a first-class degree, he worked at Magdalen College as a junior lecturer, teaching and researching medieval history. In 1960, he left Magdalen to concentrate on a career as an actor, screenwriter and playwright. Among his most acclaimed works are *The Madness of George III*, *The History Boys* and *The Lady in the Van.*

Locations: Exeter College, Magdalen College

Sir John Betjeman

Poet Laureate, writer and broadcaster Sir John Betjeman attended the Dragon School in Oxford. Many years later he became a student at Magdalen College. It is said that while at Magdalen he used to annoy his tutor C.S. Lewis by his neglect of some aspects of the curriculum. He never graduated, but did form many friendships with people such as the poet W.H. Auden during his time at Oxford. Many years later, his passion for saving heritage buildings resulted in his involvement in a campaign to save many Victorian North Oxford buildings from destruction by the university.

In 1951, he moved to The Mead in Wantage (now part of Oxfordshire), which remained the family home for many years. His wife Penelope operated the King Alfred's Kitchen in the town. There is now a blue plaque marking his life at The Mead. Following his appointment as Poet Laureate in 1972, he was awarded a honorary doctorate from Oxford University, and a fellowship at Magdalen College.

Locations: Magdalen College, Magdalen Bridge Boathouse, Wantage

Vera Brittain

Writer, pacifist and social campaigner Vera Brittain entered Somerville College in 1914, to read English literature. She stayed just one year before leaving to work as a Voluntary Aid Detachment (VAD) nurse in France, close to the front line. Vera's brother and her fiancé, as well several close friends, died in battle. After the end of the First World War, she returned to Oxford, having changed her subject to modern history with the aim of trying to understand the causes of the conflict. Her memoir, *Testament of Youth*, is regarded as one of the greatest portraits of life during the First World War, with its initial print run selling out within a day. Somerville College Library holds many of the papers acquired during the writing of an authorised biography of Vera Brittain.

In 2008, the BBC broadcast a documentary on Vera Brittain, and this was followed in 2014 by a film version of *Testament of Youth*. Scenes from the film were shot in Merton College (used to represent Somerville), Exeter College, Brasenose Lane and Radcliffe Square.

Locations: Exeter College, Merton College, Radcliffe Square, Somerville College

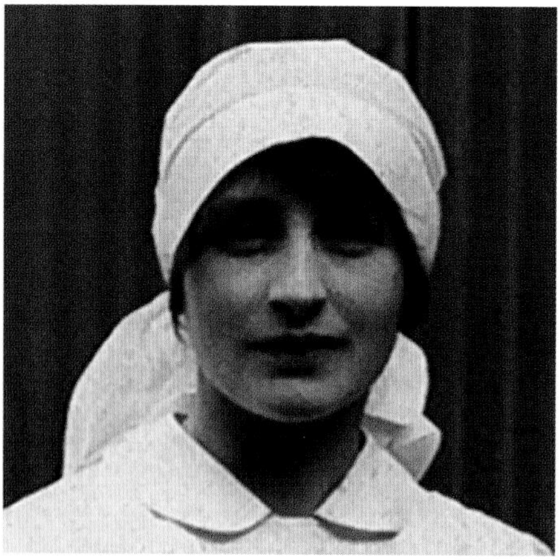

▲ ***Vera Brittain.*** (Wikimedia Commons)

John Buchan

John Buchan won a Hulme scholarship to study classics at Brasenose College. During his stay at Oxford, Buchan won essay and poetry prizes, and was elected president of the Oxford Union. Six of his works were published while at Oxford including his first adventure novels, which laid the foundation for his later writing career. His most famous novel, *The Thirty-Nine Steps*, was published in 1915 and has been filmed and reprinted on many occasions.

Location: Brasenose College

Lewis Carroll

Lewis Carroll (real name Charles Lutwidge Dodgson) was an author, poet, mathematician, photographer and Anglican deacon. He was the son of a clergyman who had studied at Christ Church, Oxford. Carroll spent much of his life as a student, before becoming a mathematics lecturer at Christ Church. He held a variety of posts during his career including sub-librarian of Christ Church Library. He enjoyed a wide range of interests including photography, the theatre and membership of the Society for Psychical Research. For many years he had a photographic studio at Christ Church where he took photographs of Alice and other children. This eventually aroused controversy, and in 1880 he stopped taking photographs.

Carroll's literary output was extensive, including stories, poems such as 'Jabberwocky' and 'The Hunting of the Snark' and mathematical puzzles. By far his most important works are *Alice in Wonderland* and its sequel, *Through the Looking Glass and What Alice Found There*.

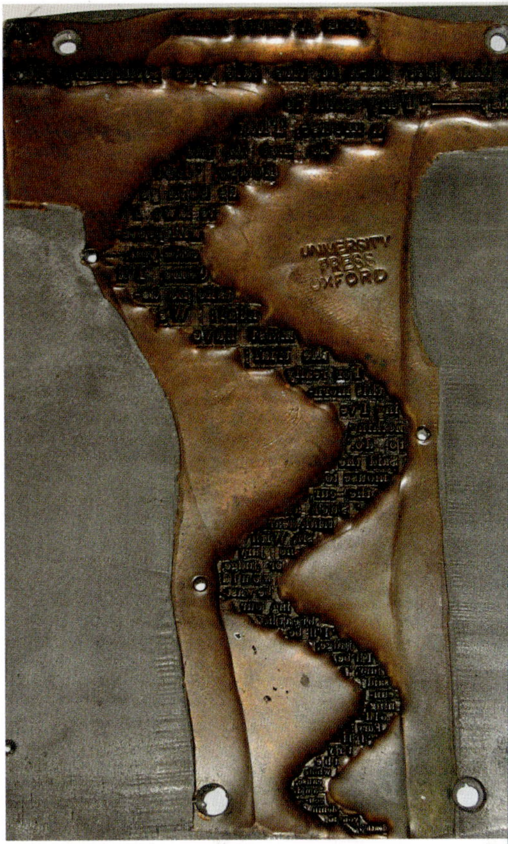

▲ ***The 'Mouse's Tail' printing plate commissioned by Carroll which presents, in the form of a tail, the poem related to Alice by a mouse in* Alice in Wonderland.** (© Oxford University Press)

The story of *Alice in Wonderland* was inspired by the young Alice Liddell, the ten-year-old daughter of the dean of Christ Church, Henry Liddell. Carroll became close friends with the Liddells, and on one occasion took Alice and her sisters on a boat trip down the Isis from Oxford to Godstone, along the way entertaining them by making up a story about a white rabbit, a red queen, a croquet game involving flamingos and hedgehogs, plus playing cards painting white roses red, which became *Alice's Adventures in Wonderland*. The story was eventually published in 1865, and

▲ ***St Margaret's Well, Binsey, described by Carroll as a 'treacle well' in* Alice in Wonderland.** (© Osney Benefice Office St Peter & St Paul)

was subsequently followed by *Through the Looking Glass and What Alice Found There* in 1871.

There are *Alice in Wonderland* walking tours around the city.

Locations: Alice's Shop, Blackwell's, Christ Church, Christ Church Cathedral, Christ Church College Gardens and the 'Alice Door', Christ Church Meadow, Godstone, Oxford Botanic Garden, Oxford Deanery, Oxford University Museum of Natural History, Port Meadow, River Isis

Geoffrey Chaucer

Often described as the father of English literature, Geoffrey Chaucer was an English poet, author, lawyer and civil servant. Born in London, his father was a wine merchant supplying the royal court. Chaucer studied law and gained various court positions such as clerk of the king's works as well as going on missions overseas on behalf of the king. Oxford was one of the places that he knew well, with his son Thomas Chaucer marrying Matilda Burghersh, whose dowry included the manor of Ewelme in Oxfordshire.

▲ ***Geoffrey Chaucer.*** (© The Huntingdon Library)

Thomas Chaucer was also constable of Wallingford Castle and was granted the manor of Woodstock by the queen.

The Chaucer crest on a helm bearing a unicorn head can be seen in St Mary's Church, Ewelme. It is believed that this was the funeral helm of Geoffrey Chaucer's son, Thomas. Geoffrey Chaucer's granddaughter Alice is buried in St Mary's Church.

A site in Oxford is mentioned in the *Canterbury Tales*: in 'The Miller's Tale', Chaucer tells the story of Alison, who has an affair with a young man named Nicholas while her carpenter husband is working at Osney Abbey, Oxford.

Locations: Osney, Ewelme, Wallingford

G.K. Chesterton

Chesterton was the author of over eighty books, hundreds of poems, short stories and plays together with a series of detective stories featuring the priest detective Father Brown. In 1911, he wrote an epic poem entitled *The Ballad of the White Horse*. It focused on the story of King Alfred and his defeat of the Danes at the battle of Ethandun. The poem began with a description of the White Horse and how it had been seen in ages past. He placed the Battle of Ethandun within the Vale of the White Horse even though there was no evidence for this location.

Location: Uffington

Agatha Christie

Agatha Christie has become the best-selling crime novelist of all time, especially with regard to her Hercule Poirot and Miss Marple stories. Her books have sold over 2 billion copies in English and translated versions. She wrote sixty-six detective novels and fourteen short story collections, plus the world's longest-running play – *The Mousetrap*.

Agatha Christie was born in 1890 in Torquay, and subsequently lived in London and Wallingford. Throughout her life she travelled extensively around Europe and to archaeological sites in Egypt and the Middle East, providing inspiration for classic stories such as *Murder on the Orient Express*.

Locations: Wallingford, Winterbrook

Winston Churchill

Author and UK prime minister throughout the Second World War, Winston Churchill was born at Blenheim Palace just outside Oxford. As he grew up, he visited Blenheim and Oxford on many occasions. He was commissioned as a captain in the Oxfordshire Yeomanry in 1902, and over the next few years steadily rose in rank until he became a major. Many of the unit's military exercises took place in the grounds of Blenheim Palace. He wrote several non-fiction books, mainly dealing with aspects of the First and Second World Wars, as well as his memoirs. In 1953, he won the Noble Prize for Literature. Churchill is buried beside his mother and father in the churchyard of St Martin's Church in the nearby village of Bladon.

Literary links: Blenheim Palace, Old Parsonage Hotel

Susan Cooper

Fantasy novelist Susan Cooper studied English at Somerville College between 1953–1955, during which time she became the first woman to edit the undergraduate newspaper, *Cherwell*. While studying at Oxford, she attended

▲ ***Winston Churchill bust and photographs at the Old Parsonage Hotel.*** (© Old Parsonage Hotel)

lectures given by both J.R.R. Tolkien and C.S. Lewis. Her most famous work is the five-part series, *The Dark is Rising*, which includes *Under Sea, Under Stone*.

Location: Somerville College

Cressida Cowell

Award-winning children's author, Cressida Cowell studied English at Keble College. As a child she loved writing and drawing stories. In 2019 she became the Children's Laureate, while in 2021 she was elected a Fellow of the Royal Society of Literature. She has written several children's book series including the *Tiny Detectives*, *The Wizards* and The *Emily Brown* books. Her best known series is *How to Train Your Dragon* which has sold millions of copies worldwide and was turned into a film series by DreamWorks Animation. She has taken part in the Oxford Literary Festival and given talks at The Story Museum which has also held an immersive 'Here be Dragons' exhibition co-curated by Cressida and Toothless.

Locations: Keble College, The Story Museum

▲ ***'Here be Dragons' exhibition, curated by Cressida Cowell and Toothless, at the Story Museum.***
(© The Story Museum)

Edmund Crispin

Edmund Crispin was the pen name of writer and composer Robert Bruce Montgomery, who graduated from St John's College in 1943. While studying at St John's he was an organ scholar and choirmaster. As a writer, he made his name as the author of classic crime stories and became a member of the Detection Club in 1947. Many of his complex stories feature locked-room mysteries.

His detective novels feature an Oxford don named Gervase Fen, who is an English professor and fellow of a fictional college named St Christopher's – which is sited adjacent to St John's College. It is believed that the character was partly inspired by W.G. Moore, a don at St John's. The Sheldonian Theatre features in the crime novel *The Moving Toyshop*. The Bodleian Library contains an archive of Robert Bruce Montgomery's correspondence.

His work as a composer includes scores for nearly forty films as well as orchestral and church music. In 1951, the Oxford Bach Choir commissioned him to write *An Oxford Requiem*. This was performed at the Sheldonian that same year, and the choir of St John's recorded the final movement entitled 'Lord, thou hast been our refuge'.

Locations: Bodleian Library, Sheldonian Theatre, St John's College

Roald Dahl

Children's author Roald Dahl spent the last years of his life in Oxford, and died there in 1990. His books include *Charlie and the Chocolate Factory*, *Matilda*, *Fantastic Mr Fox* and *The BFG*. The film *Wonka* is based on *Charlie and the Chocolate Factory* and was partly filmed in Oxford, featuring the Bridge of Sighs (Hertford Bridge), the Bodleian Library, Merton Street and the Sheldonian Theatre.

Locations: Bodleian Library, Bridge of Sighs (Hertford Bridge), Merton Street, Sheldonian Theatre, The Story Museum

Cecil Day-Lewis

Anglo-Irish poet Cecil Day-Lewis attended Wadham College. Between 1951 and 1956, he was Professor of Poetry at Oxford and was appointed Poet Laureate in 1968, partly on the advice of Oxford University's Merton Professor of English, Dame Helen Gardner, who commented that Cecil Day-Lewis 'produced run of the mill poetry but nothing particularly outstanding'. Apart from poetry, Day-Lewis is known for his series of detective novels written under the pseudonym of Nicholas Blake, featuring amateur detective Nigel Strangeways. Written in the 1930s these form part of the classic 'Golden Age' of crime fiction. Like Day-Lewis, Strangeways is portrayed as being Oxford University educated, and a literary scholar.

The Bodleian Library contains Day-Lewis's literary archive including correspondence with other poets and writers of the period.

Locations: Bodleian Library, Wadham College

Thomas De Quincey

Thomas De Quincey joined Worcester College, Oxford in 1803 and became an essayist, writing widely on subjects such as history, economics and psychology. He is best known for his book *Confessions of an English Opium Eater*. This is based on his experience of taking opium, a practice he began while at Worcester College. Initially he used opium to relieve the pain of facial neuralgia, but soon became addicted, taking ever-increasing doses of laudanum (tincture of opium).

Location: Worcester College

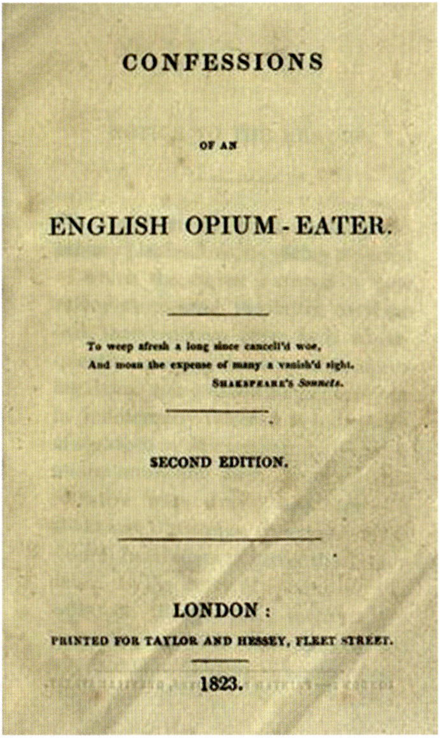
CONFESSIONS

OF AN

ENGLISH OPIUM-EATER.

To weep afresh a long since cancell'd woe,
And moan the expense of many a vanish'd sight.
SHAKSPEARE'S *Sonnets*.

SECOND EDITION.

LONDON:
PRINTED FOR TAYLOR AND HESSEY, FLEET STREET.
1823.

▲ **Confessions of an English Opium Eater.** (Wikimedia Commons)

Colin Dexter

Colin Dexter's involvement with Oxford began in 1966, having previously studied at Cambridge University. He

▲ ***Colin Dexter's portrait in 'Colin's Corner' at the Old Parsonage Hotel.*** (© Old Parsonage Hotel)

spent many years working as a teacher at schools in Northamptonshire and Leicestershire. Forced by the onset of deafness to seek an alternative occupation, he became senior assistant secretary to the University of Oxford Delegacy of Local Examinations (UODLE) between 1966 and 1988. In 2001, he was awarded the Freedom of the City of Oxford and in 2005 he became a fellow by special election of St Cross College. He died in Oxford in 2017 and a memorial service was held in Christ Church Cathedral.

An award-winning crime writer, Dexter is renowned for his creation of Inspector Morse, a detective with a love of cask ale, classical music and cryptic crosswords. His thirteen Morse novels are: *Last Bus to Woodstock* (1975), *Last Seen Wearing* (1976), *The Silent World of Nicholas Quinn* (1977), *Service of All the Dead* (1979), *The Dead of Jericho* (1981), *The Riddle of the Third Mile* (1983), *The Secret of Annexe 3* (1986), *The Wench is Dead* (1989), *The Jewel That Was Ours* (1991), *The Way Through the Woods* (1992), *The Daughters of Cain* (1994), *Death is Now My Neighbour* (1996) and *The Remorseful Day* (1993). He also produced a short story collection, *Morse's Greatest Mystery* (1993), also

▲ ***Filming* The Remorseful Day *in Oxford.*** (Wikimedia Commons/Creative Commons/Guillaume de la Mouette)

published under the title *As Good as Gold*. All the books are set in Oxford.

Between 1987 and 2000, the character of Inspector Morse was turned into a popular TV series involving thirty-three two-hour episodes. The series featured Inspector Morse, played by John Thaw, and his sidekick, Sergeant Robert Lewis, played by Kevin Whately. Dexter made a cameo appearance in almost all the episodes. In *The Daughters of Cain*, the Pitt Rivers Museum is the location of the murder weapon.

There were two spin-off series following the ending of *Inspector Morse*, both of which involved Colin Dexter as a series consultant and also various cameo appearances by him. Between 2006 and 2015, the thirty-three episode TV series *Lewis* featured Sergeant Lewis (now an inspector), again played by Kevin Whately, together with his sidekick DS James Hathaway, played by Laurence Fox. A prequel, *Endeavour*, explored the early years of Morse's career in the police force. *Endeavour* starred a young Morse played by Shaun Evans, with his senior officer played by Roger Allam. There were nine series of the programme, broadcast between 2012 and 2023.

Colin Dexter locations: Christ Church Cathedral, Ewert Place, Summertown (where Dexter worked at the University of Oxford delegacy of local examinations), St Cross College

Morse, Lewis *and* Endeavour *locations: Ashmolean Museum, Blackwell's, Brasenose College, Chipping Norton, Corpus Christi College, Exeter College, Merton College, New College, Old Bookbinders Ale House, Oriel College, Oxford Canal, Oxford Castle, Pembroke College, Pitt Rivers Museum, Port Meadow, Radcliffe Camera, Randolph Hotel, River Cherwell, St Aldegate's Street, St Mary Magdalene church, St John's College, Trout Inn, Worcester College, University College, Victoria pub, White Horse pub Marston, Wolvercote, Woodstock*

Charles Dickens Jr

The eldest son of author Charles Dickens created two handbooks relating to Oxford. One was a guidebook to the University of Oxford giving details of colleges, expenses and scholarships as well as excursions to local sites such as Osney, Blenheim, Nuneham and Woodstock. The other, published in 1879, was *Dickens's Dictionary of the Thames, From Oxford to the Nore: An Unconventional Handbook*, which was a practical guide for anyone using the river, providing details of tide tables, angling clubs, rowing sites and places along its banks. It was reprinted every year until the author's death in 1896.

Locations: Blenheim, Nuneham, Osney, Rivers Isis and Cherwell, Woodstock

John Donne

Poet John Donne studied at Hertford College, but as a Catholic he left early so as to avoid taking the oath of allegiance to Queen Elizabeth I. Despite this he was awarded an honorary masters degree in 1610 based on his poetry and prose, such as 'Pseudo-Martyr', a tract explaining why Catholics should take an amended form of the oath. By 1610, he had been ordained as an Anglian priest. His poetry includes works such as 'No Man is an Island', which includes the words, 'Never send to know for whom the bells tolls; it tolls for thee'.

Location: Hertford College

▲ ***T.S. Eliot lecture theatre, Merton College.*** (Wikimedia Commons)

T.S. Eliot

T.S. Eliot was awarded a scholarship to Merton College in 1914 where he studied philosophy. Although he only stayed a year at the university, it provided an opportunity to meet influential authors like Ezra Pound. He was not happy in Oxford, preferring to live in London, and wrote 'I hate university towns and university people, who are the same everywhere, with pregnant wives, sprawling children, many books and hideous pictures on the walls ... Oxford is very pretty, but I don't like to be dead.' Despite this, Merton College subsequently named one of its lecture theatres after Eliot and holds an annual T.S. Eliot international summer school at the college. Eliot's works include *Murder in the Cathedral*, *The Waste Land* and 'The Love Song of J. Alfred Prufrock'. He was awarded the 1948 Nobel Prize for Literature.

Location: Merton College

James Gordon Farrell

James Gordon Farrell joined Brasenose College in 1956. Very soon after his arrival he contracted polio, resulting in treatment using an iron lung, which left him partially crippled. It is believed that this experience led him towards his subsequent writing career as he ultimately drew upon it in his novel,

The Lung. After gaining his degree in modern languages in 1960, he focused on writing, winning the Faber Prize with his novel *Troubles* and then the Booker Prize for *The Siege of Krishnapur*.

Location: Brasenose College

Helen Fielding
Best known for her novel *Bridget Jones's Diary*, author and scriptwriter Helen Fielding attended St Anne's College Oxford where she studied English. Her other books include *Cause Celeb* and *Bridget Jones: The Edge of Reason*. In 2015, the third film in the Bridget Jones series involved scenes in which her baby was christened at St Mary's Church Swinbrook, Oxfordshire.

Locations: St Anne's College, St Mary's Church Swinbrook

William Fiennes
William Fiennes attended the Dragon School between 1978 and 1983. He later graduated from Oxford University and subsequently became a fellow in creative arts at Wolfson College. He is the author of *The Snow Geese* and *The Music Room*.

Locations: Dragon School, Oxford University

Ian Fleming
James Bond creator and author of *Chitty-Chitty-Bang-Bang: The Magical Car*, Ian Fleming, was born in Oxfordshire and spent part of his childhood in the area. His grandparents moved to the village of Nettlebed, located in the Chiltern Hills between Oxford and Henley-on-Thames. They lived at Nettlebed Manor before moving to nearby Joyce Grove. During the First World War, Ian Fleming and his brother Peter spent a lot of time with their grandparents.

Joyce Grove is now a Sue Ryder hospice and closed to the public. Ian's parents lived at nearby Braziers Park between 1908 and 1914 where Ian Fleming was born in 1908.

Location: Nettlebed

John Fowles
Author John Fowles entered New College in 1947 to read French and German. His books include novels that have become classics such as *The Magus* and *The Collector*. His equally iconic *The French Lieutenant's Woman* was turned into a film in 1981 starring Meryl Streep and Jeremy Irons.

Location: New College

Antonia Fraser
Award-winning author and historian Antonia Fraser was a pupil at the Dragon School between 1940 and 1944, later writing that 'it was so wonderful to be a Dragon girl'. During her time at the Dragon School she played Lady Macbeth. In 1950 she entered Lady

Margaret Hall, studying philosophy, politics and economics.

In 1985, she wrote a crime novel entitled *Oxford Blood*, set at the university. In the story, Jemima Shore, a journalist, is making a documentary about the exotic lifestyles of Oxford students when she discovers a mystery about a wealthy undergraduate, which leads to murder. It includes scenes describing punting on the river and visiting Oxford colleges.

Locations: Dragon School, Lady Margaret Hall

John Galsworthy

The son of a lawyer, John Galsworthy took a degree in law at New College, graduating in 1889. A year later, he was called to the Bar as a barrister specialising in marine jurisprudence. By 1897, he had begun publishing novels, including *From the Four Winds* and *Villa Rubein* under the name of John Sinjohn. In 1906 that he wrote the first volume of what was to become the series that made his name – *The Man of Property*, part of *The Forsyte Saga*. He also wrote plays such as *The Silver Box*. In 1932 he was awarded the Nobel Prize for Literature.

Location: New College

Alan Garner

Fantasy writer, children's storyteller and folklorist Alan Garner joined Magdalen College in 1953 to study classics. During his time at Oxford, he took part in productions with the university theatrical society, co-starring alongside Dudley Moore in William Shakespeare's *Antony and Cleopatra*. Garner did not complete his degree, having decided late in 1956 that he wanted to focus on writing novels. Despite this, he always said that he felt his university experience remained 'a permanent strength through all my life'. His most famous work is *The Weirdstone of Brisingamen* set on Alderley Edge, Cheshire. Over the years, he has won numerous awards including the Carnegie Medal and the Phoenix Award, as well as an OBE. Garner has featured many times in the Oxford Literary Festival. His works have featured in exhibitions at the Bodleian Library.

Locations: Bodleian Library, Magdalen College

William Golding

Lord of the Flies author William Golding initially attended Brasenose College in 1930, to study natural science, before switching to English. He then studied for a diploma in education. In 1983, he was awarded the Nobel Prize for Literature and in 1988 was knighted for his services to literature.

Location: Brasenose

Kenneth Grahame

The Wind in the Willows author Kenneth Grahame attended St Edward's School,

▲ ***Scene from* The Wind in the Willows.**
(Wikimedia Commons)

Oxford, and wanted to attend the university but was unable to afford it. In 1908 he and his family moved to the village of Blewbury near Oxford. His son Alistair studied at Christ Church. Alistair died after being struck by a train near Oxford. Subsequently, Kenneth Grahame and his wife Elspeth moved to Pangbourne, near Reading.

Grahame is buried in Holywell Cemetery, Oxford, where his headstone reads 'To the beautiful memory of Kenneth Grahame, husband of Elspeth and father of Alastair, who passed the River on 6 July 1932, leaving childhood and literature through him more blest for all time.'

The Bodleian Library contains letters and manuscripts relating to Kenneth Grahame, including the original manuscript of *The Wind in the Willows*. He also bequeathed all royalties of his works to 'the University of Oxford for the benefit of the Bodleian Library' enabling it to obtain numerous books and manuscripts relating to children's literature.

Locations: Blewbury, Bodleian Library, Holywell Cemetery

Robert Graves

Poet, novelist and critic Robert Graves studied at St John's College after serving as a soldier in the First World War. He studied English language and literature, and although he failed his BA degree he gained a BLitt by submitting a dissertation. This enabled him to become a teacher, but he became most well known for his writing which included a very successful biography of T.E. Lawrence, *Lawrence and the Arabs*, and his own autobiography, *Goodbye to All That*, which focuses on his early life and experiences during the First World War. Graves produced over 140 works during his lifetime, particularly translations and innovative studies of Greek myths. Many of his works, including *The White Goddess* and *Goodbye to All That*, have never been out of print. By far his most popular

▲ ***Robert Graves's house at Islip.*** (Wikimedia Commons)

book is *I, Claudius*, which was made into a TV series broadcast in 1976.

Between 1961 and 1966, Robert Graves occupied the Chair of Poetry at Oxford University.

Locations: Islip, St John's College

Graham Greene

Graham Greene studied history at Balliol College, graduating in 1925. During his time in Oxford, he frequently visited the Lamb & Flag pub where he had a crush on the barmaid. Green later recalled in his autobiography that the barmaid had a strange beauty reminding him of the Egyptian queen Nefertiti. He wrote, 'What quantities of beer we drank in order to speak a few words with her.' It was while he was at Oxford that he began writing, publishing a poetry collection under the title *Babbling April*. After graduating with a second-class degree, Greene went on to write numerous iconic books such as *Brighton Rock*, *Our Man in Havana*, *The Ministry of Fear*, *The Honorary Consul* and *The Third Man*. Balliol College possesses an archive of letters between Green and his secretary, Josephine Reid.

Locations: Balliol College, Lamb & Flag pub

Roger Lancelyn Green

Well known for his collections of Greek and Norse mythology, Roger Lancelyn Green studied at Merton College under the aegis of C.S. Lewis. During his time at Oxford, Green took part in Oxford University Dramatic society plays and was deputy librarian at Merton College for five years. He attended meetings of the Inklings literary group. Green gained a B.Litt degree. He remained a close friend of C.S. Lewis and was one of the first to read the Narnia books. When Lewis began writing the Narnia series in the late 1940s, Green recommended that they should be called *The Chronicles of Narnia*. He subsequently wrote a biography of C.S. Lewis as well as of J.M. Barrie and Andrew Lang, together with books about Lewis Carroll. Green became a founder of the Lewis Carroll Society.

Locations: Merton College, The Eagle & Child pub

Mark Haddon

Haddon was educated at Merton College, where he studied English before becoming a novelist and children's author. His most famous work is *The Curious Incident of the Dog in the Night-Time*, which won the Whitbread Best Novel and Book of the Year award in 2003. The book was written in Oxford. It has been adapted as a stage play. Other books include *The Pier Falls* and *The Red House*. He continues to live and work in Oxford.

Location: Merton College

Thomas Hardy

Thomas Hardy based his novel *Jude the Obscure* on a fictional version of Oxford, known as Christminster. The story is centred around the relationship of Jude, who has been rejected by the University of Christminster, and Sue Brideshead, a social outcast due to her views. On arrival in the city, Jude lives 'on inexpensive terms in the modest type of accommodation he demanded; and after inquiry took a room in a suburb nicknamed Beersheba'. It is generally believed this is based on the area known as Jericho.

Location: Jericho

Deborah Harkness

American author and academic Deborah Harkness studied at Keble College and visited the Bodleian on many occasions as part of her studies.

Her fantasy novel, *A Discovery of Witches*, has been adapted into a TV series. It focuses on the character of Diana Bishop, a historian and reluctant witch studying at Oxford and incorporates many Oxford locations. The most important are the Bodleian Library where Diana discovers the mysterious enchanted Ashmole 782. She regards it as a sanctuary.

Bishop holds a research fellowship at All Souls College, while vampire scholar Matthew Clairmont has been a member of the college for centuries. Throughout the series, the college forms the backdrop for numerous academic and supernatural events. Its architecture is described in the books as resembling 'the love child of a wedding cake and a cathedral, with its airy spires and delicate stonework'.

The Oxford Botanic Garden is where Diana and Matthew relax and spend time together, while The Eagle and Child pub is where they meet and discuss their research with other supernatural beings.

The Radcliffe Camera is used as a location for more academic discussions and research. Other key locations are:

- New College: Diana walks along New College Lane and then through the back gate into the college, passing the chapel windows and its garden.
- Blackwell's bookshop is where Diana goes for tea.

- The Pitt Rivers Museum is Matthew's favourite place where he can often be seen looking at the skeleton of an iguanodon and a likeness of Darwin.
- The Covered Market is where Diana goes shopping, buying venison and rabbit from the butcher and Scottish salmon from the fishmonger.
- The Bridge of Sighs (Hertford Bridge) – there are references to a vampire sitting on the curved expanse of the bridge spanning New College Lane between the two sides of Hertford College.

Oxford provides many of the filming locations for the film series, including exterior shots of the Radcliffe Camera, exterior scenes at Exeter College, the Folly Bridge over the Thames, Brown's Café, The Covered Market, All Souls College, New College, Blackwell's bookshop and the Bridge of Sighs.

In series two, Phoebe's office exterior is located in the History of Science Museum, beside the Sheldonian Theatre. There are also shots of the exterior of the Randolph Hotel.

Locations: All Souls College, Blackwell's, Bodleian Library, Bridge of Sighs, Brown's Café, Eagle and Child pub, Exeter College, Folly Bridge, History of Science Museum, Keble College, New College, Oxford Botanic Garden, Pitt Rivers Museum, Radliffe Camera, Randolph Hotel, Sheldonian Theatre, The Covered Market

Hazel Holt

Author Hazel Holt wrote detective novels, one of which involved an Oxford location. *The Cruellest Month* features Sheila Malory visiting Oxford to research wartime women writers in the Bodleian, but then finds herself investigating the murder of a librarian crushed under collapsed bookshelves.

Location: Bodleian Library

Gerard Manley Hopkins

Victorian poet and Jesuit priest Gerard Manley Hopkins studied classics at Balliol College between 1863 and 1867. It was while he was studying in Oxford that he converted to Catholicism. He later served as a priest at St Aloysius Church, Oxford, and in 1878 became

▲ ***Gerard Manley Hopkins***

a founding member of the Newman Society for Catholics studying at Oxford.

Locations: Balliol College, St Aloysius Church

A.E. Housman

Poet A.E. Housman won an open scholarship to St John's College in 1877 where he studied classics. Although he won a first in classical moderations in 1877, his lack of interest in history and philosophy meant that he failed his finals and had to return to resit the exam, resulting in a lower-level pass degree. He wrote a book on Propertius, which was rejected by Oxford University Press in 1885. During his life he wrote many poems, the most important of which was the cycle of 63 poems known as *A Shropshire Lad*.

Location: St John's College

▲ ***A.E. Housman, 1894.*** (Wikimedia Commons)

Thomas Hughes

In *Tom Brown's Schooldays*, Thomas Hughes created a semi-autobiographical novel about life at Rugby School. This was followed by the less well known *Tom Brown at Oxford* in which Tom notes that the fictional St Ambrose College falls far short of the academic rigour to which he was accustomed at Rugby: 'First and foremost it's an awfully idle place; at any rate, for us freshmen. Fancy now, I am in twelve lectures a week of one hour each – Greek Testament, first book of Herodotus, second *Aeneid*, and first book of Euclid! Two hours a day, all over by twelve, or one at the latest; and on extra work at all, in the shape of copies of verses, themes or other exercises.' It partly reflects Hughes's own experiences. Born in Uffington, he attended Rugby School and then Oriel College where he played cricket for the university team. After graduating, Hughes entered the legal profession and became a queen's counsel.

Location: Oriel College

Michael Innes

Michael Innes is the pen name of John Innes Mackintosh Stewart, best known for his crime fiction. He studied English literature at Oriel College, graduating with a BA in 1928. After teaching at Leeds University and the University of Adelaide in South Australia, he returned to the UK and eventually became a fellow of Christ Church, and subsequently a professor of the university. As Michael Innes, he wrote over fifty crime novels including stories featuring Sir John Appleby, a Scotland Yard detective inspector. His book *Death at the President's Lodging* was based in a fictional Oxford college located near Bletchley, while in *Operation Pax*, most of the action takes place in Oxford involving a fictional college known as St Bede.

Under his own name he wrote numerous books including studies of Rudyard Kipling, Thomas Love Peacock, James Joyce and Joseph Conrad.

Locations: Christ Church, Oriel College

P.D. James

Detective novelist P.D. James was born in Oxford, the daughter of a local tax inspector. She began writing during the 1950s, creating the character of Adam Dalgliesh, a New Scotland Yard investigator. Her first novel was *Cover Her Face*, which led to the creation of a series of books, while she was also working in the Civil Service. In 1991, she became a life peer with the title of Baroness James of Holland Park.

Locations: Binsey, Port Meadow

Samuel Johnson

The famous eighteenth-century lexicographer and author of *A Dictionary of the English Language* (1755), Samuel Johnson, attended Pembroke College for a short time. Lack of funds meant that he had to leave without graduating and seek employment as a teacher and writer. It took him nine years to research and write his dictionary, which has been

◂***P.D. James with actor Roy Marsden playing police detective Adam Dalgleish.*** (© Craig Davies)

▲ ***Samuel Johnson.*** (Wikimedia Commons)

acclaimed as 'one of the greatest single achievements of scholarship'. In 1755, the University of Oxford awarded him a degree of Master of Arts, followed in 1775 with a honorary doctorate. In 1776, Johnson returned to Pembroke College with his friend James Boswell and toured the college, recalling his early life at Oxford.

Location: Pembroke College

Andrew Lang

Prolific Victorian author Andrew Lang is well known for his collections of fairy tales such as *The Blue Fairy Book* (1889) and *The Lilac Fairy Book* (1910).

He gained a first-class degree in classics at Balliol College in 1868, and

▲ ***Andrew Lang.*** (Wikimedia Commons)

▲ ***Olive Fairy Book.*** (Wikimedia commons public domain)

was a fellow of Merton College between 1868 and 1875.

Locations: Balliol College, Merton College

Philip Larkin

Poet and novelist Philip Larkin studied at Oxford, gaining his BA from St John's College. Due to poor eyesight, he was not called up to serve in the Second World War and spent three years studying at Oxford, graduating in 1943. He obtained a first-class honours degree. Many of his poems were published in the student magazine *Cherwell*. After graduating he trained as a librarian, and spent most of his working life at the Brynmor Jones Library, University of Hull. During his lifetime, he published numerous poems focusing on emotions, places and relationships and was offered, but declined, the role of Poet Laureate in 1984. He edited *The Oxford Book of Twentieth Century English Verse*. He was offered the position of Oxford Professor of Poetry but declined. A letter from him later found in the safe at St Hugh's College Oxford stated that he was honoured to be asked, but was unfitted for the job due to the 'dreaded sherry drill with important people'. In 2003, the Poetry Book Society survey named him Britain's best loved poet of the past fifty years. The Bodleian Library possesses several collections of letters linked to Philip Larkin. His novel *Jill* refers to a scene in Oxford's Covered Market and its maze of stalls.

Locations: Bodleian Library, St Hugh's College, St John's College, The Covered Market

T.E. Lawrence

Born in Caernarfonshire, T.E. Lawrence moved with his family to Oxford in 1896. He attended the City of Oxford High School and subsequently began by reading law followed by history at Jesus College between 1907 and 1910. For much of the time while studying at Jesus College, he lived at the family home but, in 1908, he moved to staircase V on the First Quad of

▲ ***T.E. Lawrence in 1918.*** (Wikimedia Commons)

Jesus College. His bedroom is now a college meeting room, known as the T.E. Lawrence Room. During his time at Oxford, Lawrence did not take part in college sports or literary societies but did spend time cycling around the Oxfordshire countryside visiting village churches.

Lawrence developed a passion for archaeology, which was fuelled by the many artefacts on display in the Ashmolean Museum and Bodleian Library. As a teenage boy, he had monitored building sites in Oxford, collecting items for the Ashmolean. In 1906, the Ashmolean's annual report noted that he had 'by incessant watchfulness secured everything of antiquarian value which has been found'.

He was awarded a 'senior demy' at Magdalen College, providing financial support while undertaking further research and seeking academic status. Lawrence spent his time as a senior demy working as an archaeologist in Carchemish, Syria. With the outbreak of the First World War, his career took a different turn as he became involved in wartime operations in the Middle East. After the war he wrote an autobiographical account of his activities, *Seven Pillars of Wisdom*.

A portrait of Lawrence dating from 1928 hangs in the hall at Jesus College. A blue plaque can be seen on the outside of his childhood home at 2 Polstead Road, Oxford.

Locations: Ashmolean Museum, Bodleian Library, Jesus College, 2 Polstead Road

John Le Carré

John Le Carré was the pseudonym of David John Moore Cornwell, who read modern languages at Lincoln College, graduating with a first-class honours degree. It was while studying at Oxford that he began serving with M15 following a meeting with George Leggatt at nearby Woodstock. He was involved in the identification of double agent Kim Philby.

▲ ***John Le Carré.*** (Wikimedia Commons)

Many of his books are influenced by his time at Oxford, with the character of George Smiley being partly inspired by the Rev. Vivian Green, rector of Lincoln College. Other stories such as *Our Kind of Traitor* draw on the many influences he experienced as an Oxford undergraduate, since this book features an Oxford academic who becomes involved in an intelligence plot. Oxford locations such as the Bodleian feature in several of the novels. The filming of *Tinker, Tailor, Soldier, Spy* also took place in Oxford and involved scenes at the Bodleian, Clarendon Quad, Broad Street and Northmoor Road.

The Bodleian Library contains the John Le Carré literary archive, covering 90 metres of shelving. On donating the archive to the Bodleian, Le Carré wrote, 'Oxford was Smiley's spiritual home, as it is mine.'

Locations: Bodleian Library, Lincoln College, Woodstock

C.S. Lewis

Clive Staples Lewis came up to Oxford in 1917 having won a scholarship to study at University College. His studies were interrupted by war service in France, before returning and graduating in 1922 with a double first in greats (classical philosophy and history), followed a year later by a first in English. He was elected a fellow of Magdalen College in 1925, working as a tutor in English language and literature. He remained at Magdalen until 1954 when he took up the role of Professor of Medieval and Renaissance Literature at Cambridge University.

During his time at Oxford he lived in rooms in the New Building of Magdalen College overlooking the deer park and Addison's Walk. He attended services in the college chapel and preached in the University Church of St Mary the Virgin as well as attending his parish church, Holy Trinity at Headington Quarry. The Kilns, Headington, was his home from his undergraduate days to his death.

He was a familiar sight at places such as the Bodleian Library, accompanying Tolkien on walks along the river bank, and visiting the Lamb & Flag and The Eagle and Child pubs where he was a member of the Inklings literary group.

Between 1949 and 1954 Lewis was inspired to write the *Chronicles of Narnia*. During the Second World War, he had offered a home to evacuee children from the London Blitz, and it was these children that provided the inspiration for the Peter, Edmund, Susan and Lucy in *The Lion, the Witch and the Wardrobe*. The *Chronicles of Narnia* have become classics of children's literature, drawing on inspiration from Christian themes, Greek and Roman mythology and British and Irish fairy tales. Several

▲ ***C.S. Lewis among undergraduates at University College, 1917.*** (Wikimedia Commons)

sites in Oxford such as the Narnia Door in St Mary's Passage and the cloisters at Magdalen provided inspiration for various scenes. Over 100 million copies of the *Chronicles* have been sold worldwide and translated into over 40 languages. The series has been adapted many times for radio, TV, stage and cinema.

Other famous works include *The Screwtape Letters*, *The Space Trilogy*, *Mere Christianity* and *The Problem of Pain*.

C.S. Lewis is buried in the cemetery of Holy Trinity Church and flowers are frequently placed on his tombstone.

Locations: Addison's Walk, Ampleforth Arms Headington, Bodleian Library, Christ Church Meadow, Eagle and Child pub, Eastgate Hotel, Holy Trinity Church Headington Quarry, Lamb & Flag pub, Magdalen College, 10 Old High street Headington, Sheldonian Theatre, St Mary's Passage, The Kilns Headington, University Church of St Mary the Virgin, University College

Penelope Lively

A Booker Prize winner, Penelope Lively has written many novels and short story collections for adults and children. She was a student at

St Anne's College Oxford. Some of her children's books such as *The Ghost of Thomas Kempe* and *A Stitch in Time* are set in the Cotswold countryside.

Location: St Anne's College

Thomas Lovell Beddoes

A nineteenth-century poet, Beddoes's most important work was the dramatic poem *Death's Jest-Book; or, the Fool's Tragedy*, published in 1850. He was a student at Pembroke College when he wrote a blank verse drama called *The Bride's Tragedy*, based on the story of a murder committed by an undergraduate.

Location: Pembroke College

Compton Mackenzie

Compton Mackenzie graduated from Magdalen College with a degree in modern history. He went on to become a leading novelist, actor and writer, creating memorable stories such as *Whisky Galore*, *The Monarch of the Glen*, and *The Four Winds of Love*. He also put his experience of Oxford life to use in his novel *Sinister Street*. Max Beerbohm noted that the story 'gives you the actual Oxford experience. What Mackenzie has miraculously done is make you feel what each term was like.'

Location: Magdalen College

Rose Maculay

Rose Macaulay (1881–1958) was educated at Oxford High School for Girls before reading modern history at Somerville College. A novelist, she is best known for her award-winning novel *The Towers of Trebizond* which tells the story of a small group of Anglo-Catholics crossing Turkey by camel. It is believed to be her spiritual autobiography, reflecting her own changing beliefs. She was made a Dame Commander of the British Empire in 1957.

Location: Somerville College

Faith Martin

Faith Martin is the pen name of author Jacquie Walton, who was born in Oxford. Walton trained as a secretary and worked at Somerville College before turning her attention to writing, using various pen names of which Faith Martin the crime novelist is the most well known. Martin has sold over 2 million books worldwide. Her most popular series are the Ryder and Loveday mystery novels set in 1960s Oxford and the DI Hillary Greene series, also based in Oxford. Throughout her novels there are frequent references to all the main buildings in Oxford, particularly the various colleges and the Bodleian Library. She has taken part in the Oxford Literary Festival.

Locations: Bodleian Library, Bridge of Sighs, Oxford Canal, Somerville College

Guillermo Martinez
An Argentinian novelist and short story writer, Guillermo Martinez gained a PhD in mathematical logic at the University of Buenos Aires. He then spent two years working in a postdoctoral position at the Mathematical Institute, Oxford. His Oxford experiences subsequently led him to base two of his novels in the city, *The Oxford Brotherhood* and the hugely successful *The Oxford Murders*, written in 2003. This novel has since been translated worldwide. The story, set in Merton College, involves two mathematicians who are trying to stop a serial killer. *The Oxford Murders* was later made into a film starring Elijah Wood, with scenes being filmed in Broad Street and Blackwell's. The White Horse pub was used both as a set and as a place where extras, crew and actors stopped for a drink.

Locations: Blackwell's bookshop, Broad Street, Mathematical Institute, Merton College, White Horse pub Marston

John Masefield
Poet and author John Masefield moved to Boars Hill with his family in the 1920s. There he wrote of some of his most famous works such as *Reynard the Fox*, *The Midnight Folk*, *The Box of Delights*, *The Bird of Dawning* and *The Square Peg*. His play, *The Coming of Christ*, was the first to be performed in an English cathedral since the Reformation.

Masefield was given a honorary doctorate of literature by the University of Oxford and in 1923 organised the Oxford Recitations, a competition to identify good speakers of verse. In 1930, he was appointed Poet Laureate and remained in post until his death in 1967.

Location: Boars Hill

John Masterman
Born in 1891, John Cecil Masterman read modern history at Worcester College. Having taken a position as an exchange lecturer at the University of Freiburg, he was interned as an enemy alien when the First World War broke out, spending the next four years in a prisoner of war camp at Ruhleben. At the end of the war, he returned to the UK and became a tutor in modern history at Christ Church. While working at Oxford, he wrote two crime novels, both set in the city: *An Oxford Tragedy* and *The Case of the Four Friends*. When war broke out in 1939, he became involved in British intelligence and the Twenty Committee, responsible for the Double-Cross System of turning German agents into double agents working for the British. After the war, he returned to Oxford. In 1946, he became provost of Worcester College, and vice chancellor of the university. In 1972, he published a historical account of the Double-Cross System in the war of 1939 to 1945.

Locations: Christ Church, Worcester College

Val McDermid

Val McDermid is a graduate of St Hilda's College. After graduating she became a journalist and best-selling crime novelist. Her work has been translated into more than forty languages. Many of her books fall into the sub-genre of 'tartan noir'. Typical series include *Wire in the Blood* and *The Distance Echo*, which were subsequently adapted for television. Val McDermid has been a member of the prestigious Detection Club since 2000. Ten years later she won the CWA Diamond Dagger for her contribution to crime writing.

She is also a broadcaster, participating in a wide range of programmes including *Question Time, Have I got News For You* and *University Challenge*.

In 2023, McDermid was awarded the honorary degree of doctor of letters at Oxford. She has returned to the city frequently throughout her writing career, attending the Mystery & Crime Conference at St Hilda's where she has been given a honorary fellowship.

Oxford features in her novels *Trick of the Dark* and *The Skeleton Road*. St Scholatica's College is a combination of St Hilda's and Lady Margaret Hall. Other references include punting on the river.

Locations: River Isis, St Hilda's College

The Mitford sisters

During the 1930s and 1940s the Mitford sisters were among the most celebrated – and scandalous – society figures. All six were brought up in Oxfordshire, mainly at Asthall Manor, Swinbrook, before moving to a newly-built home in the same area. A journalist is reported to have described them as 'Diana the Fascist, Jessica the Communist, Unity

▲ ***Nancy, Diana, Unity and Jessica Mitford.*** (Wikimedia Commons)

the Hitler-lover, Nancy the Novelist, Deborah the Duchess and Pamela the unobtrusive poultry connoisseur.' Nancy wrote many books and biographies including *Love in a Cold Climate* and *The Pursuit of Love*, while Jessica wrote *The American Way of Death*. Deborah Mitford, Duchess of Devonshire, also wrote numerous books relating to Chatsworth House as well as her memoirs of being the youngest Mitford sister. Diana's book, entitled *A Life of Contrasts*, highlights her life at Asthall Manor. Unlike her sisters, Pamela stayed in Swinbrook, caring for the estate until she married.

Author Jessica Fellows wrote a series of six mystery novels in which the three oldest sisters (Nancy, Pamela and Diana) are the major characters, with other family members in supporting roles, all helping to solve mysteries. The novels are *The Mitford Murders*, *Bright Young Dead*, *The Mitford Scandal*, *The Mitford Trial*, *The Mitford Vanishing* and *The Mitford Secret*. Diana Mitford also featured in the BBC TV series *Peaky Blinders*, which showed Diana and her husband, the fascist Oswald Mosley, involved in political action.

Locations: Asthall Manor, Swinbrook

Geoffrey of Monmouth

A twelfth-century writer and cleric born in Wales, Geoffrey of Monmouth moved to Oxford in 1129 and became a canon at St George's Chapel and College at Oxford Castle. It is believed that he wrote *The History of the Kings of Britain* during his stay in the city. This book includes stories about King Arthur and Merlin, and helped establish the myth of King Arthur. According to Geoffrey of Monmouth, the book was translated from an 'ancient book in the British language that told in an orderly fashion the deeds of all the kings of Britain', which had been given to him by Walter, archdeacon of Oxford.

Location: Oxford Castle

Sir Thomas More

Tudor statesman, lawyer, philosopher, saint and author Sir Thomas More rose to prominence under Henry VIII. As a young man, he spent two years studying classics at Oxford. There are two locations that are linked to him, both of which are now defunct: Canterbury College (the site of which was later acquired by Christ Church), and St Mary Hall (acquired by Oriel College). During the reign of Henry VIII, Sir Thomas More took on many public offices including becoming high steward of Oxford University in 1524. His most famous work is *Utopia*, describing a society in which there is no private property, but there is universal religious toleration, plus free education for both men and women. Refusing to accept Henry VIII as head of the Church in England, he was executed. There is a chapel dedicated to him in Foxcombe Road, Boars Hill, Oxford, as well as in the Oxford University Chaplaincy at The Old Palace, Rose Place, St Aldate's.

Locations: Boars Hill, Christ Church, Oriel College, Oxford University Chaplaincy

William Morris

Textile designer, artist and author of early fantasy novels such as *The Well at the World's End*, *The Roots of the Mountains* and *The Wood Beyond the World*, William Morris joined Exeter College in 1852. During his time at Oxford, he developed an interest in medieval history, inspired by the medieval buildings found throughout the city. After graduating he began working with the Oxford-based architect George Edmund Street, before moving to London. Eventually he moved into textiles and painting, and helped Rosetti and Burne-Jones complete the Arthurian murals in the Oxford Union. His work helped revive traditional crafts and textiles, as well as establishing the fantasy genre. He founded Kelmscott Press as a publisher of illuminated print books. The William Morris Society is devoted to his legacy. He lived for many years at Kelmscott Manor, Kelmscott, Oxfordshire.

▲ ***William Morris, age 53.*** (Wikimedia Commons)

Locations: Exeter College, Kelmscott, Oxford Union, Uffington

Ian Morson

Born in Derby, Ian Morson won a scholarship to University College Oxford in 1965 where he studied Russian. During his time in Oxford, he regularly performed folk music at the city's pubs. Morson's medieval detective, Master William Falconer, is regent master at the fictional Aristotle's Hall, part of the University of Oxford. Morson also writes stories as part of the Medieval Murderers Group. His contribution to the anthology *The Tainted Relic* refers to Osney Abbey, Oxfordshire.

Locations: Osney Abbey, University College

Iris Murdoch

A prolific author with twenty-six novels to her name, Iris Murdoch attended Somerville College, Oxford where she studied classics. She became a fellow of St Anne's College, where she taught philosophy until 1963. A Booker Prize winner, her novels include *The Italian Girl, The Sandcastle, Under the Net, The Nice and the Good* and *The Black Prince*. There is a bench dedicated to her in the grounds of Lady Margaret Hall. Her home was in Charlbury Road, Summertown, North Oxford and is marked by a blue plaque. Merton Street and Magpie Lane were used as locations during the filming of *Iris*, the 2001 film about her life.

Locations: Charlbury Road Summertown, Lady Margaret Hall, Magpie Lane, Merton Street, Somerville College, St Anne's College

V.S. Naipaul

Born in Trinidad and Tobago, Naipaul won a scholarship to Oxford in 1950 where he attended University College. Naipaul studied English and when he graduated in 1953, J.R.R. Tolkien

▲ **Iris Murdoch studying at St Anne's College copyright St Anne's College.** (Report-readingjpg)

commented that his Anglo-Saxon paper was the best in the university. Naipaul later said that he 'hated Oxford'. His novels mainly focus on his Trinidadian background and include *A House for Mr Biswas*. Naipaul was awarded the Nobel Prize for Literature in 2001.

Location: University College

S.J. Parris

S.J. Parris is the pen name of Stephanie Merritt, and under this pseudonym she has written a series of historical novels featuring a real-life sixteenth-century heretic, philosopher and spy known as Giordano Bruno. There are seven books in the series: *Heresy*, *Prophecy*, *Sacrilege*, *Treachery*, *Conspiracy*, *Execution* and *Alchemy*. *Heresy* is set in Oxford during 1583, featuring the hero Giordano Bruno, who is working undercover at the university and investigating a series of murders. Bruno stays at Lincoln College as a guest of the rector. The real Giordano Bruno was born in Italy, later working in Toulouse, Paris and London. In 1583, he gave a series of lectures at Oxford promoting the work of Copernicus and the movement of the Earth around the Sun. He was also due to take part in an academic disputation with the rector of Lincoln College, chaplain to Queen Elizabeth I. A contemporary note by Gabriel Harvey referred to Bruno as being able to 'argue most readily about every conceivable matter'. His views were greeted with considerable hostility and he returned to London and the court of Elizabeth.

Location: Lincoln College

Walter Pater

Victorian writer Walter Pater studied Greek philosophy at The Queen's College, Oxford. In 1864 he was elected to a fellowship at Brasenose College during which he wrote extensively on art history, particularly Renaissance art. This brought him into contact with the Pre-Raphaelites. His most famous work is *Marius the Epicurean*, a philosophical romance set in ancient Rome. He is buried in Holywell Cemetery.

Locations: Brasenose College, Holywell Cemetery, The Queen's College

Philip Pullman

Best known for the *His Dark Materials* and *The Book of Dust* trilogies, Philip Pullman attended Exeter College where he studied English, graduating in 1968. Many years later, during an interview with the *Oxford Student*, he commented that he had not really enjoyed his English course and that, 'I thought I was going quite well until I came out with my third class degree and then I realised that I wasn't – it was the year they stopped giving fourth class degrees otherwise I'd have got one of those.' He became a teacher in Summertown, North Oxford,

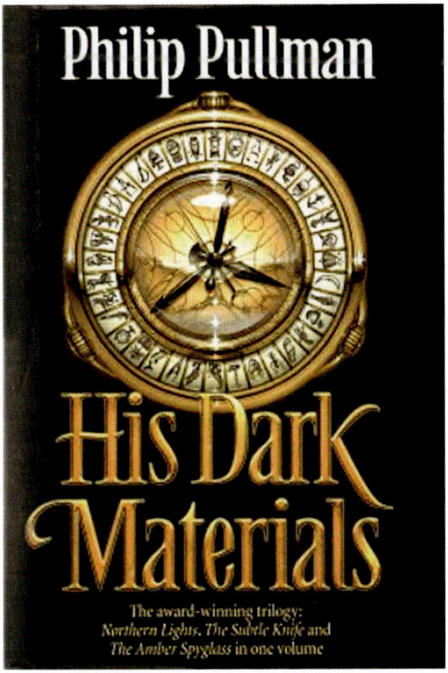

▲ **His Dark Materials.** (© Philip Pullman)

later moving to Westminster College, Oxford, where he taught part-time while developing his writing career. In 2004, he was elected an honorary fellow of Exeter College. In 2009, the University of Oxford awarded him a doctor of letters during a ceremony at the Sheldonian Theatre.

Oxford has provided the major inspiration for the setting of *His Dark Materials*. The character, Lyra Belacqua, grows up at Jordan College, which is based on Oxford's Exeter College, while Lyra and Will Parry agree to meet annually at the Botanic Garden. This garden is based on the Oxford Botanic Garden, nestling beside the River Cherwell. The bench they agree as a meeting place is located at the back of the garden.

The Bodleian Library becomes Bodley's Library, a repository for the alethiometer, while The Covered Market, with its narrow alleys and countless small shops, is reflected in market scenes. Although not specifically mentioned in the books, the Pitt Rivers Museum provided inspiration for artefacts such as the alethiometer described in Pullman's novels.
A museum of this type is where Lyra investigates the 'Tartar phenomenon' of trepanned skulls in *The Subtle Knife*.

Port Meadow is portrayed in *La Belle Sauvage* (the first volume in *The Book of Dust* trilogy), with Malcolm Polstead taking a canoe ride with the infant Lyra along the flooded river. It is also the site of the horse fair in *Northern Lights* where a young boy from 'a gyptian family she knew' triggers Lyra's subsequent adventures. Jericho is where the gyptians board their boats in *Northern Lights*, and is also where action is located in *La Belle Sauvage*.

Just outside Oxford, the ruins of Godstow Abbey are depicted as being a refuge and place of sanctuary for both Malcolm Polstead and the infant Lyra Belacqua as they flee from dangerous forces during a flood. The Trout Inn, Wolvercote, is the inspiration for the pub in which Malcolm lives with his parents in *La Belle Sauvage*.

The stories have been the subject of films and a BBC TV series. Among the filming locations used are Exeter College, New College, The Queen's College, the Bridge of Sighs, Oxford Botanic Garden and Christ Church Meadow.

Locations: Bodleian Library, Bridge of Sighs, Christ Church Meadow, Exeter College, Godstow Abbey, Jericho, New College, Oxford Botanic Garden, Pitt Rivers Museum, Port Meadow, River Cherwell, Sheldonian Theatre, The Covered Market, The Queen's College, The Trout Inn Wolvercote

Barbara Pym

Barbara Pym read English at St Hilda's College and subsequently wrote many novels, mostly satires about suburban life such as *Quartet in Autumn*. Her novel *Crampton Hodnet* is set in North Oxford, and includes the reference, 'It was a wet Sunday afternoon in North Oxford at the beginning of October. The laurel bushes which bordered the path leading to Leamington Lodge, Banbury Road, were dripping with rain' and later notes that 'heaven might be something like North Oxford'.

Between 1972 and 1980, she lived at Barn Cottage, Finstock. A blue plaque now marks the site. She is buried in Finstock churchyard.

Locations: St Hilda's College, Finstock

Sir Arthur Quiller-Couch

Poet and novelist Sir Arthur Quiller-Couch was educated at Trinity College. Between 1886 and 1887, he was lecturer in classics at Trinity after which he moved to London. During his writing career he wrote numerous novels and short stories such as *Dead Man's Rock* as well as compiling various poetry anthologies including the *Oxford Book of English Verse*. He was a honorary fellow of Trinity College.

Locations: Trinity College

J.K. Rowling

Joanne Rowling, better known as J.K. Rowling, the best-selling author of the *Harry Potter* novels, applied to study English literature at Oxford University in 1982 but was rejected. She subsequently opted for the University of Exeter. The *Harry Potter* series focuses on the activities of a boy wizard attending Hogwarts, a school for wizards, and his battles with the evil Lord Voldemort, involving choices between good and evil. The series became a global sensation selling over 600 million copies, and has been translated into eighty-four languages. It has also led to the creation of numerous video and board games as well as a film series.

Oxford was extensively used as a film location for the *Harry Potter* films, especially *Harry Potter and the Philosopher's Stone* (2001), *Harry Potter*

▲ ***Christ Church Hall provided the inspiration for Hogwarts Great Hall*** (© David Hawgood)

and the Chamber of Secrets (2002), *Harry Potter and the Prisoner of Azkaban* (2004) and *Harry Potter and the Half-Blood Prince* (2009).

The Bodleian Library features in many scenes. The scene in which Harry walks through Hogwarts Library hidden under the invisibility cloak was filmed in the Bodleian's Duke Humfrey's Library. Hermione is seen studying in this library on many occasions. Another area of the library known as the Divinity School was used as the Hogwarts Infirmary in *Philosopher's Stone*. At the end of the film, Harry is shown lying in bed talking to Dumbledore after his confrontation with Voldemort. In *Goblet of Fire*, it was used to film the students practising dancing for the Yule Ball where Ron dances with Professor McGonagall. A scene in *Half-Blood Prince* shows Ron in the Infirmary after being accidentally poisoned. Standing outside the Old Bodleian Library is a bronze statue of William Herbert, 3rd Earl of Pembroke, which is believed to have inspired Rowling to create the ghostly character of Nearly Headless Nick, who appears in several films.

New College Cloisters and courtyard houses the gigantic oak tree under which Mad Eye Moody turns Malfoy into a ferret in *Goblet of Fire*. It is also where Harry seeks out Cedric Diggory to talk about the dragons in the first task.

Christ Church was frequently used in filming. Its central staircase was used during the arrival of Harry, Ron and Hermione at Hogwarts when they first meet Professor McGonagall. It also features in scenes in *Chamber of Secrets* when Harry is 'inside' Riddle's Diary. The Great Dining Hall, dating from Tudor times, was the inspiration for the Hogwarts Dining Hall complete with feasts and the Sorting Hat. It was recreated as a permanent film set which can now be seen at the Warner Brothers Harry Potter Studio Tour, Watford.

Christ Church cloisters covered walkways acted as a location for scenes set in the hallways of Hogwarts', such as that where Hermione shows Harry the Quidditch trophy won by his father.

The site outside the Sheldonian Theatre is where Rowling was inspired to create Harry's lightening-bolt scar. She had been asked by her publisher to create a clearer idea of the scar, and while exploring Oxford saw the mason's mark on one of the flagstones.

The Turf Tavern is where the Harry Potter cast and crew used to hang out after filming sessions.

'The Harry Potter tree' is located in the grounds of Blenheim Palace and was used to film the scene where Harry watches Snape's memories in *Order of the Phoenix*. Snape is seen reading by the tree, and is bullied by James Potter while Lily watches.

Locations: Blenheim Palace, Bodleian library, Christ Church, Divinity School, New College, Sheldonian Theatre, Turf Tavern

John Ruskin

Having graduated from Christ Church, Ruskin was a supporter of the Pre-Raphaelites as well as a prominent author. He can only be described as a polymath when it came to writing, as he covered a wide range of subject matter including literature, travel, history, art, architecture, geology, botany and education. Typical titles include *Modern Painters* (a defence of the work of artist J.M.W. Turner), *The Seven Lamps of Architecture* and *The Stones of Venice*. In 1869, he became the first Slade Professor of Fine Arts at the University of Oxford, and created the Ruskin School of Drawing in 1871 (now the Ruskin School of Art). Ruskin influenced the design and decoration of the Oxford University Museum of Natural History, and the Ashmolean holds his teaching collection of notes, catalogues and instructions.

▲ ***John Ruskin.*** (Wikimedia Commons)

Locations: Ashmolean Museum, Christ Church, Ruskin School of Art, Oxford University Museum of Natural History

Siegfried Sassoon

War poet Siegfried Sassoon was invalided to Somerville College in 1916 following the Somme offensive. He later returned to Oxford in 1919 when he lived in Merton Street. During the inter-war years, he lived in Oxford and involved himself in Labour politics. In 1965, he received an honorary degree from Oxford University.

Locations: Merton Street, Somerville College

Dorothy L. Sayers

An acclaimed 'Golden Age' detective writer and author of a series of mysteries featuring Lord Peter Wimsey, Dorothy L. Sayers was born in Oxford. Her father was headmaster at Christ Church Cathedral Choir School and a chaplain at the cathedral. Her birthplace in Brewer Street is marked with a blue plaque. She was a student at Somerville College and graduated with first-class honours in modern languages. Sayers then went to work for the publisher, Blackwell. Her novel *Gaudy Night* features many

▲ ***Cover of* Gaudy Night.** (Wikimedia Commons)

Oxford locations including Somerville (the inspiration for Shrewsbury College), Christ Church, where Lord Peter Wimsey's nephew is a student, Wimsey's own college of Balliol, Radcliffe Camera where Harriet Vane tries to work, and St Cross Church which links to Peter and Harriet who hire a punt at Magdalen Bridge Boathouse.

Locations: Balliol College, Brewer Street, Christ Church, Magdalen Bridge Boathouse, Radcliffe Camera, Somerville College

Vikram Seth

Born in 1952, Vikram Seth is an Indian poet and novelist. He attended Corpus Christi College where he studied politics, philosophy and economics, graduating in 1975. His published works include *The Golden Gate*, *From Heaven Lake*, *Mappings* and *Summer Requiem*.

Location: Corpus Christi College

Dr Seuss

American children's author Dr Seuss (Theodore Seuss Geisel) was a graduate student at Lincoln College, studying for a DPhil in English literature. It was here that he met his wife, Helen Palmer, who encouraged him to change direction from teaching to becoming an artist. He returned to America in 1927 without completing his studies. He subsequently wrote numerous best-selling children's books such as *The Cat in the Hat* and *How the Grinch Stole Christmas*, many of which have since been turned into animated films.

Location: Lincoln College

William Shakespeare

William Shakespeare stayed in Oxford when travelling between London and Stratford-upon-Avon. He was friendly with the Crown Tavern's innkeeper John Davenant and according to legend was linked romantically to John's wife Jane. Shakespeare was godfather to their son, William Davenant and there were rumours that William Davenant was

▲ ***William Shakespeare.*** (Wikimedia Commons)

actually Shakespeare's illegitimate son. The remains of the Crown Tavern still exist, hidden behind the eighteenth-century facade of No. 3 Cornmarket. Known as the 'Painted Room', it comprises a fourteenth-century timber framed room complete with oak panelled walls and Elizabethan wall paintings.

Location: No. 3 Cornmarket

Percy Bysshe Shelley

Nineteenth-century poet Percy Bysshe Shelley came to Oxford in 1810 and attended University College. His time at Oxford was short, as he was expelled the following year. According to the College Register, he was 'contumaciously refusing to answer questions proposed to him'. In 1815, Shelley returned to Oxford with his mistress Mary Shelley and friend Lord Byron and there are records of the trio enjoying a boating excursion on the river. The Bodleian Library contains works by Shelley, created while he was a student at Oxford. There is also a statue of Shelley and a Shelley library in the Bodleian.

Locations: Bodleian Library, Shelley statue, University College

▲ ***Shelley memorial.*** (© University College Oxford)

Sir Philip Sidney
Poet and sixteenth-century courtier Sir Philip Sidney attended Christ Church. His works include the first treatise of literary criticism in English, *An Apology for Poetry*, and the first modern prose romance, *English Arcadia*.

Location: Christ Church College

Robert Southey
Poet Robert Southey was educated at Balliol College. He recalled that he arrived with 'a heart full of poetry and feeling, a head of Rousseau and Werther, and my religious principles shaken by Gibbon', but that 'All I learnt was a little swimming ... And a little boating.' During his time in Oxford, he visited The Trout Inn with his friends. Among his most famous works are the poem 'After Blenheim' and the original version of 'Goldilocks and the Three Bears.'

▲ ***Robert Southey.*** (Wikimedia Commons)

Locations: Balliol College, The Trout Inn

Stephen Spender
A poet and novelist who focused on social injustice, Stephen Spender studied at University College where he became friends with W.H. Auden and Christopher Isherwood. He left Oxford in 1929 without taking a degree, and later commented that he had never passed any exams. He was made a honorary fellow of University College in 1973. Journals and drafts of his work are archived in the Bodleian Library.

Locations: Bodleian Library, University College

Veronica Stallwood
Author of a series of mystery books set in Oxford, Veronica Stallwood lives in Charlbury, Oxfordshire. She has worked at the Bodleian Library and Lincoln College Library. Her novels feature mysteries mainly focusing on unnamed Oxford colleges and an Oxford publishing house. The central character is novelist and amateur sleuth Kate Ivory. In *Oxford Exit*, Ivory investigates book thefts from the Bodleian Library.

Locations: Bodleian Library, Lincoln College, Charlbury

Rosemary Sutcliff
Sutcliff was a major children's author of legends, myths and historical stories particularly relating to prehistory, the Iron and Bronze ages and the Romano-British frontier period. She was well known for researching her books with care, aiming for accuracy with regard to her chosen periods. She was a runner-up for the Hans Christian Anderson Medal. In 1977, Sutcliff wrote *Sun Horse, Moon Horse* which included references to the White Horse of Uffington. Illustrator Shirley Felts used a picture of the White Horse on the book's cover.

Location: Uffington

Jonathan Swift
Eighteenth-century writer Jonathan Swift wrote, 'I had the honour to be for some years a student at Oxford.' In reality his time at Oxford was brief. He entered Hart Hall (now Hertford College) in 1692, and matriculated the same year. Obtaining a degree was an important step for him, since without it he could not be ordained as a clergyman. He is most well known for his novel *Gulliver's Travels*.

Location: Hertford College

Algernon Swinburne
Victorian poet Algernon Swinburne attended Balliol College between 1856 and 1860, but never graduated with a degree. In 1859, he was sent down (rusticated) due to his public support for the attempted assassination of Napoleon III. While at Oxford, he was involved with the Pre-Raphaelite movement, especially Dante Gabriel Rossetti and William Morris. A lyrical poet, his works include *Atalanta in Calydon*, *Poems and Ballads*, *Chastelard, a Tragedy*, *Tristram of Lyonesse* and *The Queen-mother, and Rosamond*.

Location: Balliol College

Ann Swinfen
Educated at Somerville College, Ann Swinfen read classics and mathematics, later studying for a PhD in English literature. In the 1990s she became a full-time writer focusing on historical novels. These include a Fenland series based in seventeenth-century East Anglia, and a series of Oxford mysteries set in the fourteenth century. The Oxford mysteries feature bookseller Nicholas Elyot and his university friend Jordain Brinkylsworth and their encounters with crime. Titles include *The Bookseller's Tale*, *The Novice's Tale* and *The Troubadour's Tale*. Oxford made an impression on her as she indicates in The History Blog, as she refers to memories of walking down the tiny Magpie Lane in winter, Merton chapel, punting on the river, the Broad and Carfax. Holywell Mill, where her character Miller Wooten lived, was also

familiar to her as she recalled cycling there once a week for a tutorial.

Locations: Carfax, Holywell Mill, Magpie Lane, Merton College, River Cherwell, Somerville College, The Broad

Dylan Thomas

Poet and author Dylan Thomas and his wife visited Oxford in Autumn 1945 when they stayed with friends Margaret and A.J.P. Taylor at their home, Holywell Mill, in the grounds of Magdalen College. They became regular visitors and in March 1946 moved into the summerhouse in the grounds of Holywell Mill. Their daughter lived in the main house with Margaret and Taylor's family while Dylan Thomas and his wife camped out in the summerhouse. Conditions were a little basic, as there were no facilities like water, gas or electricity. Despite this, they stayed there until 1947. During this time, Thomas socialised a lot and met with undergraduates at popular pubs like the Turf Tavern, The Trout at Wolvercote, The Perch at Binsey and The George Hotel in Wallingford. On 8 February 1948 he broadcast an episode of *Country Magazine* for the BBC from The Fleece at Witney.

Thomas wrote of his stay in Oxford:

Oxford I sing, though in untutored tones, alack!
I heard, long years ago, her call but blew it back:
... Ah not for me the windblown scarf,
The bicycle to the Trout, the arm-in-arm sweatered swing,
Marx in a punt, Firbank aloud round the gas-ring.
Never in flannelled and umbrella'd youth did I
Tire of the sun with talking and drive him down the High.

Locations: Holywell Mill, Randolph Hotel, Turf Tavern, The Fleece Witney , The George Hotel Wallingford, The Perch Binsey, South Leigh

Charles Todd

Charles Todd is the pen name of mother and son, Caroline and Charles Todd. They created a series of detective novels, including one involving Inspector Ian Rutledge set in the early 1920s. In Volume 10 of the Rutledge series, the Inspector is searching for the identity of a man found dead in Fountains Abbey, Yorkshire. His search leads him to the village of Uffington where people are hiding from their own pasts.

Location: Uffington

J.R.R. Tolkien

Tolkien is one of the most well-known authors linked to Oxford due to his works *The Hobbit* (1937) and *The Lord of the Rings* (1954–1955).

In 1911, he went up to Oxford to study classics at Exeter College. He

▲ ***J.R.R. Tolkien in First World War uniform.*** (Wikimedia Commons)

quickly discovered he didn't enjoy the subject and switched to English language and literature, graduating in 1915 with a first-class honours degree.

After serving in the army during the First World War, he returned to Oxford to work with Oxford University Press on the *Oxford English Dictionary*, and was based at the Old Ashmolean Museum in Broad Street – now the History of Science Museum. It was a key period in his life, as he later noted he had 'learned more in those two years than in any other equal part of his life'. After a short stay at Leeds University as reader in English Language, he returned to Oxford in 1925 as Professor of Anglo-Saxon at Pembroke College.

It was while he was marking examination papers that he discovered a candidate had left a blank page. It inspired Tolkien to write the immortal words 'in a hole in the ground there lived a hobbit' – from this he eventually created his stunning imaginary world. He remained at Pembroke until 1945. He lived at 20 Northmoor Road between 1930 and 1937, and it was there that he wrote much of *The Lord of the Rings*.

Between 1945 and 1959, Tolkien was Professor of English Language and Literature at Merton College. During these years, he often wrote outdoors on the old stone table located in the gardens. Many Tolkien specialists believe this may have been the inspiration for Elrond's conference

▲ ***'Speak Friend and Enter'.*** (© The Story Museum)

table in *The Fellowship of the Ring*. There is also a hobbit-sized door in the grounds.

Although he and his wife Edith retired to Poole in Dorset for a few years, Tolkien moved back to Oxford after her death in 1971 when he took up residence as a Merton College emeritus fellow.

Radcliffe Camera provided the inspiration for Sauron's temple to Morgoth in Nümenor, while the Bodleian Library contains the Tolkien archive of manuscripts and original drawings. It also contains the fifteenth-century *Red Book of Hergest* which was bound in red leather and is a compilation of Welsh history and poetry, which provided the inspiration for Tolkien's *Red Book of Westmarch*.

The Oxford Botanic Garden was one of his favourite spots and provided inspiration for the trees that came alive as Ents.

The Ashmolean Museum contains many artefacts that would have been familiar objects to Tolkien, especially a cabinet containing gold finger rings possessing a short inscription on their surface.

The Eagle and Child pub was a familiar drinking place for Tolkien and his friends, especially C.S. Lewis and other members of the Inklings literary group. Tolkien was a regular member between 1933 and the late 1950s when he stopped attending.

The Rollright Stones, located at Chipping Norton, Oxfordshire, are thought to have provided inspiration for the creation of the Barrow Downs, in which the hobbits are ensnared by a barrow-wight in *The Lord of the Rings*.

Tolkien and his wife Edith are both buried at Wolvercote Cemetery. Their grave is marked by a stone bearing the names Lúthien and Beren, characters from *The Silmarillion* and *The Lord of the Rings*, whose lifelong love was reflected by that of Tolkien and his wife.

Locations: Ashmolean Museum, Bodleian Library, Exeter College, History of Science Museum (Old Ashmolean), Merton College, Merton Street, Northmoor Road, Oxford Botanic Garden, Oxford University Press Museum, Pembroke College, Radcliffe Camera, River Cherwell, Rollright Stones, The Eagle and Child pub, Wolvercote Cemetery, Uffington

Simon Tolkien

The grandson of J.R.R. Tolkien, Simon Tolkien attended the Dragon School, Oxford. He graduated from Trinity College in 1972 having studied modern history. He became a barrister in London. Since 2001, he has been a full-time writer, and has written crime stories featuring Inspector Trave of the Oxford police. Titles include *Final Witness*, *Orders From Berlin* and *The Inheritance*. His wartime tale *No Man's Land* partly reflects his grandfather's experiences during the First World War, with the central character Adam

Raine studying for a degree at Oxford University before heading to war.

Locations: Dragon School, Trinity College

Joanna Trollope
In 1961 Joanna Trollope won a scholarship to St Hugh's College where she studied English. After graduating, she worked for the Foreign Office and then entered teaching. She began writing historical fiction and by 1980 was a full-time author with books including *Britannia's Daughters* and *Parson Harding's Daughter*. Her work evolved into contemporary fiction, some of which has been adapted for TV. She donated her archives and handwritten manuscripts to the Bodleian Library. Her book *The Men and Girls* uses Oxford's Covered Market as a location for an attempted reconciliation between the main characters.

Locations: Bodleian Library, St Hugh's College, The Covered Market, Turf Tavern

Evelyn Waugh
Best known as the author of *Brideshead Revisited*, Evelyn Waugh studied at Hertford College. He later wrote that he wasted his time at Oxford. Waugh had originally aimed to go to New College, but was offered a place as a history scholar at Hertford, graduating in 1922. He later wrote that Hertford was a 'respectable but rather dreary little college'. He lived in ground floor rooms in Old Buildings Quad. In *Brideshead Revisited*, the story begins in Oxford where the lead characters Sebastian Flyte and Charles Ryder become friends while studying at Oxford. Scenes from the TV adaptation of the book were shot in Christ Church and Hertford.

Locations: Christ Church, Hertford College, The Trout Inn Wolvercote

John and Charles Wesley
Founder of the Methodist Church, and author of many books relating to the scriptures, John Wesley attended Christ Church, where he was ordained a deacon in 1725. He subsequently became a fellow of Lincoln College. His brother Charles, a notable hymn writer, also attended Christ Church. The two brothers began a regular schedule of

▲ ***Oxford Castle prison*** (© Continium)

studies in 1729 at Oxford, regarded by Wesley as 'the first rise of Methodism', including social work at the Oxford Castle prison.

Locations: Christ Church, Lincoln College, Oxford Castle

Oscar Wilde

Oscar Wilde joined Magdalen College in 1874 to study classics, claiming that it was the course of study 'where one can be, simultaneously, brilliant and unreasonable'. He wrote that life in Oxford was 'extravagance, trivial talk, utter vacancy of employment'. Despite this attitude, his studies flourished and he won the prestigious Newdigate Prize for his poem 'Ravenna', ultimately graduating with a double first.

Location: Magdalen College

Charles Williams

Novelist, poet and theologian Charles Williams was a member of the Inklings and friendly with both C.S. Lewis and J.R.R. Tolkien. He joined the staff of Oxford University Press in 1908 and stayed there until his death in 1945. *The Silver Stair*, his first book of verse, was published in 1912. Over the next thirty-three years he produced anthologies, poetry, plays, literary criticism, fiction, biographies and books relating to theology. Williams was also interested in the occult and mankind's struggle against demons, subjects which influenced some of his written work. His fantasy books include *War in Heaven and Many Dimensions*. C.S. Lewis ranked his poems on King Arthur and the Holy Grail as being particularly good due to the 'soaring and gorgeous novelty of their technique and their profound wisdom'.

Locations: Jericho, Oxford University Press, The Eagle and Child pub, Walton Street

2

KEY LOCATIONS

OXFORD CITY CENTRE

ADDISON'S WALK
Magdalen College
High Street Oxford
OX1 4AU
www.magd.ox.uk

This picturesque 1.3 km footpath around a small island in the River Cherwell and through the grounds of Magdalen College offers views of Magdalen Tower and Magdalen Bridge. It is named in honour of Joseph Addison, a seventeenth-century fellow of the college who enjoyed walking along the route. In the twentieth century, C.S. Lewis (also a fellow of the college) frequently used this walk along with his friends J.R.R. Tolkien and Hugo Dyson. It was one of Lewis's favourite walks and was the location of the evening walk in 1931 when the trio discussed metaphor and myth, leading to Lewis's conversion to Christianity. Lewis also wrote a poem focusing on Addison's Walk entitled 'Chanson d'Aventure' or 'What the Bird Said Early in the Year'. A plaque near the entrance to Holywell Ford commemorates the poem.

Addison's Walk is a free access public footpath.

Literary Links: C.S. Lewis, J.R.R. Tolkien

ALICE'S SHOP
83 St Aldate's Street
Oxford
OX1 1RA
www.aliceinwonderlandshop.com

This small Grade II* listed building will forever be linked to the story of Alice Liddell and Lewis Carroll. Alice Liddell lived directly opposite in Christ Church where her father was dean and she used to buy her sweets at the shop. The building dates back to the fifteenth century, although it was remodelled two centuries later. Lewis Carroll featured the shop as 'The Old Sheep Shop' in *Alice Through the Looking Glass*, in which an old sheep sits knitting. Nowadays, the store trades as 'Alice's Shop', selling Alice-themed gifts, souvenirs and memorabilia.

Literary Links: Alice in Wonderland, Lewis Carroll, Colin Dexter, Julian Herzog

▲ ***Alice's Shop.*** (© Mark Davies, Alice's Shop)

ASHMOLEAN MUSEUM
Beaumont Street
Oxford
OX1 2PH
www.ashmolean.org

The Ashmolean Museum is considered Britain's first public museum, and forms one of the four Oxford University museums that are open to the public. It opened in 1683 and initial artefacts on display included items like the dodo and Guy Fawke's lantern. Over the centuries, it has expanded to cover a vast array of exhibits including Egyptian mummies, the spectacular Alfred Jewel, samurai armour and contemporary art. The museum was a familiar destination for countless Oxford writers including Lewis Carroll and J.R.R. Tolkien. It was here that Carroll was inspired to include the dodo in his *Alice* books. T.E. Lawrence's links with the Ashmolean go back to his childhood when he took part in numerous rescue excavations and donated objects to the museum. The site also appears in many of Colin Dexter's Morse book series, and was frequently used as a filming location for all three related TV productions.

Literary Links: Lewis Carroll, Colin Dexter, T.E. Lawrence, John Ruskin, J.R.R. Tolkien

▼ ***Ashmolean Museum.*** (Wikimedia Commons/Creative Commons)

BLACKWELL'S BOOKSHOP
48–51 Broad Street,
Oxford
OX1 3BG
www.blackwells.co.uk

Founded in 1879 by Benjamin Henry Blackwell, Blackwell's bookshop still trades from its original site on Broad Street, which was originally only 3.6 metres square. The store expanded rapidly in size, becoming Oxford's leading bookshop. Benjamin Blackwell's son, Basil Blackwell, gained a scholarship to study at Merton College before joining the family business in 1913 with the task of expanding its publishing activities. Centrally located on Broad Street, Blackwell's quickly became the key supplier of books to all the university colleges, attracting students, lecturers and Oxford residents alike. Crime writer Dorothy L. Sayers worked there after graduating from Somerville. It is believed to be the largest bookshop in the world. The basement alone contains over 4.8 km of shelving containing 150,000 books. Blackwell's published J.R.R. Tolkien's first poem, 'Goblin Feet', in 1915.

Literary Links: Lewis Carroll, Colin Dexter, Guillermo Martinez, Dorothy L. Sayers

▼ ***Blackwell's in Broad Street.*** (© Geograph/Wikimedia Commons)

BODLEIAN LIBRARY
Broad Street
Oxford
OX1 3BG
www.bodleian.ox.ac.uk

The Bodleian is one of the oldest libraries in Europe, having been founded in 1602 by Sir Thomas Bodley. Possessing over 13 million printed items, it is the second largest library in the UK after the British Library. Known colloquially as the 'Bodley' or the 'Bod' it is a reference library and no documents or books can be removed from the reading rooms. Most students and lecturers will have used the Bodleian at some point and possess links to it, including Oscar Wilde, C.S. Lewis, Tolkien and forty Nobel Prize winners. Most of the books in the library are now stored underground in a network of over 160 km of corridors.

The Bodleian comprises a group of five buildings: Duke Humfrey's Library, Radcliffe Camera, Weston Library, Schools Quadrangle and the Clarendon Building. Among the treasures held

▼ ***Bodleian Library.*** (Wikimedia Commons/Creative Commons/Ozeye)

there are original works by *Wind in the Willows* author Kenneth Grahame, many of the original manuscripts of C.S. Lewis and the literary archive of John Le Carré. It was one of the filming locations for the 1993 film *Shadowlands*, which dealt with the relationship between C.S. Lewis and Joy Davidman.

Duke Humfrey's Library is the oldest of all the Bodleian buildings and is well known for its role in the *Harry Potter* films where it doubled as Hogwarts Library. It is named after Humphrey, 1st Duke of Gloucester, a younger son of Henry IV and is the oldest reading room in the Bodleian. Closing time is indicated when a bell is rung in the corner of the library.

Access to the library is only possible via pre-booked tours of the Bodleian and Duke Humfrey's Library. Book well in advance.

LITARARY LINKS: Edmund Crispin, Roald Dahl, Alan Garner, Kenneth Grahame, Deborah Harkness, Hazel Holt, Philip Larkin, T.E. Lawrence, Cecil Day-Lewis, John Le Carré, C.S. Lewis, Faith Martin, Philip Pullman, J.K. Rowling, Percy Bysshe Shelley, Veronica Stallwood, J.R.R. Tolkien, Joanna Trollope

BRASENOSE LANE

A narrow lane in the heart of Oxford city centre, Brasenose Lane runs between Radcliffe Square and Turf Street. It has a very medieval ambiance, with a single

▲ ***Brasenose Lane.*** (© Eugene Birchall/Wikimedia Commons/geograph.org.uk)

drainage channel (known as a kennel) running down the centre and tall, stone-faced buildings which form part of Brasenose College, Exeter College and Lincoln College. It is a pedestrian-only street when entered from Turf Street, but vehicles are allowed to enter via Radcliffe Square. It has appeared in many TV programmes and films, such as Vera Brittain's *Testament of Youth*.

Literary Links: Vera Brittain

BREWER STREET

Located just south of Carfax in central Oxford, this narrow street acts as a

▲ ***Brewer Street, birthplace of Dorothy L. Sayers.***
(© Owen Massey McKnight/Wikimedia Commons)

link between St Aldate's and St Ebbe's Street. Dating back to medieval Oxford, the street was originally occupied by butchers and slaughterers and called 'Slaying Lane'. Although it was sometimes known as Brewer Street and Lane from 1772 due to the presence of a brewhouse, it was not until 1932 that it officially became Brewer Street. A plaque on the wall of one of the houses indicates where crime writer Dorothy L. Sayers was born. Her father was headmaster of Christ Church Cathedral School.

Literary Links: Dorothy L. Sayers

BRIDGE OF SIGHS
New College Lane
Oxford
OX1 3BL

Also known as Hertford Bridge, the Bridge of Sighs is an iconic Oxford location. It joins two sides of Hertford College, providing a crossing over New College Lane. The bridge gained its more familiar name due to its

▲ ***Bridge of Sighs.*** (© UGA Gardner OpenVerse Flickr)

similarity to the Bridge of Sighs in Venice. A Grade II listed building, it was constructed in 1914. The bridge is a familiar sight in many TV and film productions, including *Inspector Morse*, *Lewis* and *Endeavour*.

Literary Links: Roald Dahl, Colin Dexter, Deborah Harkness, Faith Martin, Philip Pullman

BROAD STREET

Frequently referred to as 'The Broad' by local people, this wide street is home to numerous bookshops including Blackwell's, plus many major buildings such as the Sheldonian Theatre, the History of Science Museum, Balliol College, Trinity College and Exeter College. A cross of granite sits in the pavement is a memorial to the Oxford Martyrs – Protestants who were burnt at the stake in 1555, as well as Thomas Cranmer the following year. Another martyrs' memorial can be seen inside the nearby church of St Giles'. A blue plaque outside the Oxfam charity shop at 17 Broad Street marks the opening of the first ever Oxfam store. Broad Street has frequently featured in films and TV productions such as *Tinker, Tailor, Soldier, Spy*. It is the venue for many major city events such as the Christmas Light Festival and Christmas Market.

Literary Links: John Le Carré, Guillermo Martinez, Ann Swinfen

BROWN'S CAFÉ
92 The Market
Oxford
OX1 3DY
www.oxford-coveredmarket.co.uk

Brown's Café was opened in 1920 by Catherine Brown, who started the business on her own. Until recently, it was believed that Brown's started trading in 1924 but research for an exhibition marking its hundredth anniversary revealed an earlier date. The café is unusual in that it has only been run by four people, including Catherine Brown, who began trading as the sole business owner at a time when women were only just beginning to do so. It was not, however, a family business. Brown, who lived in Broad Street nearby, had previously undertaken various jobs such as a dressmaker and maid. The café provided traditional home-cooked food at a reasonable cost, and was advertised as being 'clean, comfortable and especially convenient for business people'. Over the years, Brown's expanded its site, taking over adjacent areas. In 1977, a Portuguese family took over, retaining the historic name. The café has been a popular venue for Oxford students and staff, and has featured in the novels of Deborah Harkness.

Literary Links: Deborah Harkness

▲ ***Brown's Café.*** (© Oxford City Council)

CARFAX
Queen Street
Oxford
OX1 1ET

Located at the junction of St Aldate's, Cornmarket Street, Queen Street and High Street, Carfax marks the centre of Oxford. Carfax Tower (also known as St Martin's Tower) is a Grade II listed building and originally formed part of the medieval St Martin's Church. The tower is owned by Oxford City Council and no building in central Oxford is allowed to be taller than its 23 metre height. The tower still has a ring of six bells which are sounded on special occasions, and a clock that chimes the quarter hours on a pair of bells. The tower is open daily, allowing visitors to climb the ninety-nine steps leading to the roof for spectacular views of the Oxford skyline. During one of Colin Dexter's cameo roles as a tramp, filmed from the top of tower, he was approached by a down and out, who grabbed his bottle only to find it contained water.

Literary Links: Colin Dexter, Ann Swinfen

▼ ***Carfax Tower*** (© Oxford City Council)

DIVINITY SCHOOL
Broad Street
Oxford
OX1 3AZ
www.visit.bodleian.ox.ac.uk/tours

A medieval building, this is the oldest surviving purpose-built structure in the university and is located behind the Sheldonian Theatre in the Bodleian Library. It was originally constructed as the venue for oral exams, theological discussions and student lectures on theology, hence the name Divinity School. The Divinity School is no longer used for this purpose but remains part of the university, being attached to the Bodleian Library. Duke Humfrey's Library is located directly above the school. The elaborate vaulted ceiling, complete with 455 roof bosses is quite spectacular, while Christopher Wren created the main entrance door in 1669 to provide access to the Sheldonian Theatre. The Divinity School is particularly well known for its role as the Infirmary at Hogwarts in *Harry Potter and the Philosopher's Stone*.

▲ ***Divinity School.*** (Wikimedia Commons/Creative Commons/Flikr/Cornell University Library)

Tours of the Divinity School, usually in conjunction with Duke Humfrey's Library, are extremely popular, and must be pre-booked.

Literary Links: C.S. Lewis, J.K. Rowling

EASTGATE HOTEL
76 High Street
Oxford
OX1 4BE
www.accor.com/hotel/6668

A seventeenth-century coaching inn, the Eastgate Hotel, part of the Mercure hotel chain, overlooks the Examination Schools and Magdalen Tower. It was later rebuilt in eighteenth-century style. J.R.R. Tolkien and C.S. Lewis were frequent visitors to the Eastgate Hotel.

There have been reports of ghostly Civil War Royalist soldiers passing through the walls, reflecting the fact that the site was once the old east gate to the city of Oxford.

Literary Links: Sir John Betjeman, C.S. Lewis, J.R.R. Tolkien

FOLLY BRIDGE
Abingdon Road
Oxford
OX1 4LB

Folly Bridge was erected between 1825 and 1827, and is a short walk from Christ Church. Built in two parts, it is separated by an island. There has been a stone bridge on this site since 1085, and this latest version has three arches. Part of the bridge is on the site of Friar Bacon's Study, where medieval alchemist Roger Bacon lived and worked. It was from this bridge that Lewis Carroll took the

▲ ***Folly Bridge.*** (Wikimedia Commons/Creative Commons)

Liddell children on that legendary trip down the river during which he first told the story of *Alice in Wonderland*.

Literary Links: Lewis Carroll, Deborah Harkness

HISTORY OF SCIENCE MUSEUM
Broad Street
Oxford
OX1 3AZ
www.hsm.ox.ac.uk

▲ ***Einstein's blackboard at the History of Science Museum.*** (© Museum of the History of Science / Wikimedia Commons)

Also known as the Old Ashmolean Building, this museum first opened in 1683 to house Elias Ashmole's collection of artefacts. From the beginning it was open to the public, and is the world's first purpose-built museum. The early museum included a chemical laboratory in the basement, with various lectures and demonstrations taking place on the first floor. After various major donations of collections were made during the twentieth century, the museum was renamed the History of Science Museum in 2018. It holds a major collection of scientific instruments dating from the medieval period through to the nineteenth century, as well as displays of mechanical clocks, optical instruments and early photographic items. Among its many iconic objects is Einstein's blackboard used by Albert Einstein during a lecture given at the university in May 1931. The museum is mentioned on several occasions in the Deborah Harkness books while the Old Ashmolean played a role in the work of Tolkien.

Literary Links: Deborah Harkness, J.R.R. Tolkien

HOLYWELL MILL
Mill Lane
Oxford
OX1 3UH

There has been a mill on this site since 1200. The present Grade II listed building was built in 1888. It later became a private residence, used by

▲ ***Holywell Mill.*** (© Dylan Moore/Wikimedia Commons/Creative Commons/Geograph Britain)

various university personnel. At one point, historian A.J.P. Taylor lived at the mill with Dylan Thomas as his lodger. Dylan Thomas and his wife spent a year living in the summer house, which he described as a 'converted telephone kiosk with a bed where the ledge for directories used to be'. In 1994, Magdalen College incorporated the site and used it as a graduate house.

Literary Links: Dylan Thomas, Ann Swinfen

LAMB & FLAG PUB
12 St Giles' Street
Oxford
OX1 3JS
www.lambflagoxford.com

Owned by St John's College, the Lamb & Flag pub was traditionally used to fund DPhil scholarships. The name comes from the symbol of Christ as the Lamb of God, carrying a banner with a cross. It has been trading since 1566. John's College closed it in January 2021. A year

▲ ***Lamb and Flag pub.*** (© Wikimedia commons/ geograph.org.uk)

later, it reopened as a community interest pub.

The pub has played a part in the lives of several eminent authors – Lewis and Tolkien used it, and Graham Greene is said to have visited it while studying at Balliol. Between 1962 and 1963, the Lamb & Flag was the venue for meetings of the Inklings following modernisation of The Eagle and Child. These meetings ended soon after Lewis died in 1963. There have been suggestions that the pub provided inspiration for Thomas Hardy to write part of *Jude the Obscure*, but no one knows if this is so. The Lamb & Flag has also featured in many episodes of *Inspector Morse* and *Endeavour*.

Literary Links: Colin Dexter, Graham Greene, C.S. Lewis

MAGDALEN BRIDGE BOATHOUSE
Magdalen Bridge
Oxford
OX1 4AU
www.oxfordpunting.co.uk

Located under Magdalen College Tower, at the end of Oxford High Street, is the Magdalen Bridge Boathouse. People have been able to hire rowing boats and punts from this location for many years as a way of exploring the river. Dorothy L. Sayers includes references to Lord Peter Wimsey and Harriet Vane renting a punt from the Magdalen Bridge Boathouse.

There has been a bridge on this site, linking the divided sections of the River Cherwell, for centuries. The first stone bridge appears to have been installed during the medieval period, incorporating twenty arches. When that bridge collapsed in 1772, the existing bridge was built. It contains eleven arches of varying dimensions providing both vehicular and pedestrian access. In 1882, the bridge was widened to accommodate a tramway track.

Apart from its popularity as a punting destination, the bridge is the setting for the annual May Day celebrations when people gather on

▲ ***Magdalen Bridge and punts.*** (Wikimedia Commons/Creative Commons/Geograph Britain & Ireland)

and around the bridge to hear the Magdalen College Choir singing from the top of Magdalen Tower at 6 a.m. The choir begins with a hymn, followed by a madrigal 'Now is the Month of Maying' and prayers led by the Dean of Divinity. There is a party atmosphere, with many students taking part in all-night balls before the event. By the 1980s a student-based custom had emerged involving jumping from the bridge into the river. Since the river can be shallow at times, this was dangerous and caused severe injury leading to the practice being forbidden, and the bridge closed on May morning.

During the summer, pre-booking is recommended, as demand can be high. At other times, boats and punts are readily available. A chauffeured punting service is also provided.

Literary Links: Max Beerbohm, John Betjeman, Dorothy L. Sayers

MAGPIE LANE
High Street
Oxford
OX1 4ES

A narrow lane leading from the High Street, close to Oriel College and University College, Magpie Lane leads into Grove Walk between Merton College and Corpus Christi College. It is one of the oldest streets in Oxford, and during the thirteenth century it was known as Grope Lane, since it was where prostitutes could be found. The name Magpie Lane was first used in the seventeenth century due to the presence of an alehouse bearing the symbol of a Magpie. It was used as a location during the filming of *Iris* in 2001.

▲ ***Magpie Lane.*** (Wikimedia Commons/Creative Commons)

Literary Links: Iris Murdoch, Ann Swinfen

MATHEMATICAL INSTITUTE
Radcliffe Observatory
Andrew Wiles Building
Woodstock Road
Oxford
OX2 6GG
www.maths.ox.ac.uk

The University of Oxford has a long history of mathematical study, involving mathematicians like Christopher Wren and Edmond Halley as well as Charles Dodgson (better known as Lewis Carroll) who was involved in the study of geometry. Dodgson even suggested that the university should give its mathematicians a strip of ground so that they could test whether parallel lines could ever meet. In 1930 suggestions were made to build a specific mathematics institute, but this was deemed too expensive. It was not until 1966 that a Mathematical Institute was constructed. Over the years it outgrew that building and since 2013 has been housed in the Andrew Wiles Building. The final episode of *Lewis* ('What Lies Tangled', filmed in 2015) was set and filmed in the institute. Sir Andrew Wiles (Regius Professor of Mathematics) played the role of a professor and appeared in the background.

LITERARY LINIKS: Lewis Carroll, Colin Dexter, Guillermo Martinez

MERTON STREET

This cobbled street runs roughly parallel to the High Street for much of its length, joining the Ruskin School of Art and the Eastgate Hotel. Merton and Corpus Christi Colleges can be accessed from the street, and there is also an entrance to Christ Church. In 1919, the war poet Siegfried Sassoon had rooms in Merton Street while in the 1970s J.R.R. Tolkien lived there.

Literary Links: Roald Dahl, Iris Murdoch, Siegfried Sassoon, J.R.R. Tolkien

▼ ***Merton Street, Oxford.*** (© Sandy Gemmill/Wikimedia Commons/Creative Commons/Geograph Britain and Ireland)

MUSEUM OF OXFORD
Town Hall
St Aldate's
Oxford
OX1 1BX
www.museumofoxford.org

Located in a Grade II listed building, the Museum of Oxford focuses on stories about Oxford and its history. It explores all aspects of Oxford history including its links with Morris cars, pubs and quirky customs. Among its most iconic items are personal items relating to Lewis Carroll, Alice Liddell and the *Alice in Wonderland* stories. These include Alice Liddell's red cross medal for her voluntary work during the First World War, watches that belonged to her, scissors, a card case, pencils and books as well as a pocket watch belonging to Lewis Carroll.

Literary Links: Lewis Carroll

▼***Displays at the Museum of Oxford.*** (© Museum of Oxford)

NO. 3 CORNMARKET
Oxford
OX1 3EX
www.oxfordpreservation.org.uk

Owned by Oxford City Council, this timber-framed building dates from the mid sixteenth century although the exterior now has an eighteenth-century facade. In 1600, it housed the Crown Tavern run by John Davenant and his wife Jane. One of the visitors to the Crown was William Shakespeare, who was rumoured to be the father of Davenant's son William. He was certainly his godfather. Shakespeare used the tavern as a stopping point on his journeys between Warwickshire and London. One of the most unusual features of the house are its Elizabethan wall paintings featuring beautiful flower designs. The paintings date from around 1580, and are believed to have been covered up by John Davenant. They were rediscovered in 1927. Some of the paintings were removed to the Ashmolean and later placed on the wall of the Oxford Museum. The Oxford Preservation Trust was also set up in 1927, and in the 1940s Sir John Betjeman, the trust's secretary, had his office in the Painted Room.

The Painted Room is open to the public on special occasions such as Shakespeare's birthday and during 'Heritage Open Days'. Special arrangements can also be made with the Oxford Preservation Trust.

Literary Links: William Shakespeare

OLD PARSONAGE HOTEL
1–3 Banbury Road
Oxford
OX2 6NN
www.oldparsonagehotel.co.uk

There has been a building on this site since medieval times. By 1660, it was owned by University College. The present house dates from 1639 with further changes and extensions made in subsequent centuries. In the 1870s

it provided lodgings for university students, one of whom is believed to have been Oscar Wilde. Having returned late from travels in Greece in 1877, he was suspended from Magdalen College and sought refuge in the Old Parsonage's current room 25.

It is now a luxury hotel, and featured in the filming of 'The Daughters of Cain'. It was a favourite location of Colin Dexter. One of the features of the hotel is its gallery of modern portraits including one of Colin Dexter by Celia Montague, located in the Parsonage Grill. The portrait sits above his favourite booth, lovingly referred to as 'Colin's Corner'. Elsewhere in the hotel the residents' library walls are adorned with a specially commissioned collection of Paddy Summerfield's black-and-white photographs of 1960s Oxford. The library contains a section dedicated to Oxford's literary giants including Tolkien and Lewis. The hotel

Old Parsonage Hotel. (© Dalight Historic)

also contains a life-size bust of Winston Churchill by Oscar Nemon, plus rare photographs and memorabilia of both Randolph Churchill and Winston Churchill. The bronze bust is cast from an original which was enlarged for Blenheim Palace.

Literary Links: Colin Dexter, Oscar Wilde

OSNEY ABBEY
Mill Street
Oxford

During the medieval period, this house of Augustinian canons was one of the four most important monastic houses in Oxford. It was the location of the Synod of Oxford in 1222 when St George's Day was first recognised as a holiday. The abbey is mentioned in Chaucer's 'The Miller's Tale' as being the setting for Alison to have an affair with a young man called Nicholas. It is also referred to in Hilaire Belloc's poem 'Newdigate', as well as in Charles Dickens Jr's *Unconventional Handbook*. A ruined archway from the abbey can still be seen in Mill Street, West Oxford near Oxford station.

Literary Links: Chaucer, Hillaire Belloc, Charles Dickens Jr

OXFORD BOTANIC GARDEN
Rose Lane
Oxford
OX1 4AZ
www.glam.ox.ac.uk/botanicgarden

This is the oldest botanic garden in the UK and contains over 5,000 different plant species. It was originally founded as a physic garden in 1621 with the aim of growing plants for medicinal research. Subsequent extensions led to the creation of a seventeenth-century walled garden which is home to the garden's oldest tree – an English yew. There is a lower garden area incorporating a rock garden, bog garden and a series of glasshouses focusing on alpines, ferns, insectivorous plants, tropical lilies, palms and cacti. The Botanic Garden still maintains eight

▲ ***'The Carpenter of Oxford' ('The Miller's Tale').*** (Wikimedia Commons)

▲ ***Oxford University Botanic Garden.*** (© Miranda Hodgson/Geograph/Wikimedia Commons)

flower beds containing a medicinal plant collection covering cardiology, oncology, infectious diseases, gastroenterology, dermatology, haematology, neurology and pulmonology. A separate arboretum has been created six miles away in southern Oxford.

During the 1860s, the Botanic Garden was frequently visited by Lewis Carroll and the Liddell children, and helped to inspire *Alice in Wonderland*. In Sir John Tenniel's illustration of 'The Queen's Croquet Ground', the Botanic Garden's Waterlily House is clearly seen in the background. Other literary links include J.R.R. Tolkien, Deborah Harkness and Evelyn Waugh. A bench at the back of the garden featured in Philip Pullman's *His Dark Materials* as being the site where Lyra and Will promise to visit at noon on Midsummer Day, no matter which alternate world they are in. The bench has since been inscribed by fans with graffiti bearing their names.

The Botanic Garden is open daily, but a charge is levied.

OXFORD CANAL
www.oxfordcanaheritage.org

The Oxford Canal was built in the late eighteenth century and roughly follows the route of the River Cherwell from Cropredy to Kidlington. In total it is 126 kilometres long, connecting the River Thames and the Grand Union Canal. In the Oxford area, the canal is very much a leisure destination, attracting narrowboats and walkers, especially with the existence of several canalside pubs. In Oxford, the canal offers two links to the Thames, one north of the city close to King's Lock and the other south of Isis Lock near the railway station. The Canal is featured in various TV series and novels such as Colin Dexter's Inspector Morse story *The Wench is Dead*, which is based on the true story of Joanna Franks on the canal in 1859. An annual Oxford Canal Festival is held in September featuring music, food, drink and community events, which have included Sir Philip Pullman reading live on stage.

Literary Links: Colin Dexter, Faith Martin

OXFORD CASTLE
44–46 Oxford Castle
Oxford
OX1 1AY
www.oxfordcastleandprison.co.uk

Oxford Castle has been in existence for over 1,000 years. Norman baron Robert O'Doyley built the first motte-and-bailey castle. It has been a prison since 1071, and only ended that role in 1996. Oxford Castle is believed to be where Geoffrey of Monmouth penned *The History of the Kings of Britain*. In the eighteenth century, John and Charles Wesley, together

Oxford Castle. (© Continuum Attractions)

with fellow students, visited Oxford Castle to work with the prisoners. John Wesley preached at the castle once a month.

The site was used to film parts of the *Inspector Morse* series, as well as *102 Dalmatians* featuring Glen Close. It was transformed into the 'Su Chou' prison in 2001, where Brad Pitt's character, Tom Bishop, was held captive during the film *Spy Game*.

The castle is operated by Continuum Attractions. It is open to the public and visitors can climb the Saxon St George's Tower for stunning 360-degree panoramic views, or

discover the 900-year-old crypt which is the only surviving part of St George's Chapel. A different aspect of the castle's history can be explored in the eighteenth-century Debtors' Tower and Prison D Wing.

Oxford Castle undertakes a regular programme of events and activities including a 'Jailbreak Escape' murder mystery events and a spectre ghost tour.

Literary Links: Colin Dexter, Geoffrey of Monmouth, John and Charles Wesley

OXFORD RAILWAY STATION
Park End Street
Oxford
OX1 1HS

Opened as part of the Great Western Railway network in 1844, the station is close to the site of the former Osney Abbey. Located a short distance from the city centre, it provides direct links with London Paddington and London Marylebone, Birmingham New Street, Hereford and Southampton.

Oxford station features in the novels and TV adaptations of *Inspector Morse*, *Lewis* and *Endeavour* (for example, in 'The Wench is Dead', the character of Adele is seen entering the building).

Literary Links: Colin Dexter

OXFORD UNION
St Michael's Street
Oxford
OX1 2DU
www.oxford-union.org

The Oxford Union was founded in 1823, and acts as a social hub for university students from all the colleges. It is most well known for being a debating society attracting international speakers from politics, academia and popular culture. It holds weekly debates enabling students to acquire debating and public speaking skills.

William Morris and Pre-Raphaelite artists' mural, Oxford Union Library. (Wikimedia Commons/Creative Commons)

The Old Library in the Oxford Union was originally the main debating chamber. The building is renowned for its stunning wall murals painted by William Morris, Dante Gabriel Rossetti and Edward Burne-Jones. These murals are characteristic of Pre-Raphaelite art. The murals depict scenes from Arthurian myth, such as Sir Lancelot's vision of the Holy Grail and Sir Palomides jealousy of Sir Tristan and Iseult. One of the models, Jane Burden, later married William Morris. The murals initially created problems as they were painted directly onto the walls without plaster or any underpainting and thus decayed quickly. Restoration work was essential, and William Morris later completely repainted his ceiling design.

It is possible to visit the Debating Chamber and Old Library most days. A charge is payable.

Literary Links: William Morris

OXFORD UNIVERSITY MUSEUM OF NATURAL HISTORY

Parks Road
Oxford
OX1 3PW
www.oumnh.ox.ac.uk

Opened in 1860, this is the world's first purpose-built natural history museum. The museum's Gothic architecture was influenced by the work of John Ruskin. It contains over 7 million specimens relating to the natural world, plus a massive library and archive. There is also a collection of paintings and sculptures focusing on natural history. Other exhibits include major palaeontology collections of fossils and dinosaurs. Among the highlights of the collection is the only example of the now extinct dodo. It was a popular attraction for Alice Liddell and her sisters, as well as Lewis Carroll who included it in his *Alice* stories.

The museum is free and is open daily. There is a changing programme

▲ ***Oxford University Museum of Natural History.*** (© Christopher Hilton, Wikimedia Commons/Creative Commons/ Georaph.org.uk)

of public events, exhibitions and activities.

Literary Links: Lewis Carroll, John Ruskin

OXFORD UNIVERSITY PRESS MUSEUM
Great Clarendon Street
Oxford
OX2 6DP
www.global.oup.com/uk/archives/5.html

The Oxford University Press Museum traces the history of Oxford's involvement in printing and publishing since the fifteenth century. There are displays relating to developments in printing machinery, including a nineteenth-century printing press. It explores the development of Oxford University Press over the centuries, and has displays about some of its publications such as the *Oxford English Dictionary* and King James Bible. A key area focuses on *Alice's Adventures in Wonderland*. After army service during the First World War, J.R.R. Tolkien worked on the Oxford dictionary before returning to the academic world.

Charles Williams, one of the Inklings and a fantasy novelist in his own right, also worked at Oxford University Press.

Pre-booking is essential. There is no charge, but all visits must be booked at least twenty-four hours in advance via the website. Guided tours are available. The museum is open Monday to Friday except public holidays and between Christmas and New Year.

Literary Links: Lewis Carroll, J.R.R. Tolkien, Charles Williams

▸ ***Displays at the Oxford University Press Museum.*** (© Oxford University Press Museum)

▾ ***Display showing the* Oxford Almanac *and* Oxford English Dictionary.** (© Oxford University Press)

PITT RIVERS MUSEUM
Parks Road
Oxford
OX1 3PW

The museum was founded in 1884 to house archaeological and ethnographic objects collected by General Pitt Rivers. Some artefacts were obtained during his service overseas, while the remainder were sourced at auction, via dealers and other members of the Anthropological Institute. On display are musical instruments, weapons, masks, textiles, jewellery and tools stressing diversity in solving similar problems across time and culture. The museum has several literary links including the works of Philip Pullman and Colin Dexter.

Entry to the museum is via the Museum of Natural History. There is no admission charge.

Literary Links: Colin Dexter, Deborah Harkness, Philip Pullman

PORT MEADOW
Walton Well Road
Oxford
OX2 6ED
www.oxford.gov.uk

Port Meadow is a public open space that according to local legend has never been ploughed. The right to

▼ ***Pitt Rivers Museum.*** (© Jorge Royan, Wikimedia Commons/Creative Commons)

graze animals on the meadow was first recorded in the 1086 Domesday Book. Over the centuries, it has been used for many purposes including being turned into a military aerodrome during the First World War, while in the Second World War it housed soldiers evacuated from Dunkirk. It has also been a centre for public festivals.

The extensive open space stretches from Jericho to Wolvercote and the village of Binsey. It is a popular walking and boating area. Lewis Carroll and his friend Duckworth rowed Alice Liddell and her sisters through Port Meadow in July 1862, while Lewis told the story that became *Alice in Wonderland*.

Port Meadow has featured in episodes of *Morse*, *Lewis* and *Endeavour*.

Access to Port Meadow is via Walton Well Road, Aristotle Lane and Godstow Lane.

Literary Links: Lewis Carroll, Colin Dexter, P.D. James, Philip Pullman

RADCLIFFE CAMERA
Radcliffe Square
Oxford
OX1 3BG

Built in a baroque English Palladian style between 1737 and 1749 to a design by James Gibb, the library originally

▼ ***Rowing past Port Meadow.*** (Wikimedia Commons/Creative Commons/Geograph Britain and Ireland/Des Blenkinsopp)

housed science books. In 1861, all the science books were moved elsewhere and the Radcliffe Camera became part of the Bodleian. A distinctive circular building, it is now used as a Bodleian reading room housing books from the English, history and theology collections. There is an underground tunnel comprising a two-storey book store linking it with the main Bodleian Library.

The Radcliffe Camera is one of the most iconic buildings in Oxford and appears frequently in films and TV

Radcliffe Camera. (© Julian Herzog, Wikimedia Commons/Creative Commons)

programmes. Vera Brittain's *Testament of Youth* involved filming in the adjacent Radcliffe Square. J.R.R. Tolkien used the building as inspiration for Sauron's temple to Morgoth in Númenor. Another key literary link involves crime writer Dorothy L. Sayers, who set her story *Gaudy Night* in Oxford, which includes a conversation between Lord Peter Wimsey and Harriet Vane on the rooftop of the Radcliffe Camera.

The Radcliffe Camera is not open to the public.

Literary Links: Vera Brittain, Deborah Harkness, Dorothy L. Sayers, J.R.R. Tolkien

RANDOLPH HOTEL
Beaumont Street
Oxford
OX1 2LN
www.hilton.com/en/hotels/lonrdgu-graduate

Owned by the Hilton hotel chain, the Randolph Hotel is located in the centre of the city. The hotel features in the Colin Dexter Morse novels and also in the TV versions, especially 'The Wolvercote Tongue' (based on the novel *The Jewel That Was Ours*), which involves Morse investigating the death of an American hotel guest. Morse and Lewis are often seen discussing their cases in the Randolph Bar with Morse commenting, 'They serve a decent pint.' Various crime suspects from the series have also been portrayed as staying at the Randolph. Colin Dexter himself often appeared as an extra in scenes set in the bar.

The cast stayed at the hotel during filming in 1987. The hotel was later used in the *Lewis* series. The Morse Bar reflects the links between the hotel and the detective series. Colin Dexter actually wrote some of the books in the bar. A portrait of John Thaw as Inspector Morse can be seen above the fireplace.

Built in Victorian Gothic style, the hotel was named after Dr Francis Randolph, a university benefactor who was involved with the Ashmolean Museum, rather than Randolph Churchill, the father of wartime leader Winston. Although the hotel was well known to Randolph Churchill, who had been brought up in the nearby Blenheim Palace and studied for a degree at Merton College, Oxford, his links were a little more dramatic since it is reported that he smashed its windows while an undergraduate.

The hotel also features in Osbert Lancaster's illustrations for Sir Max Beerbohm's novel *Zuleika Dobson*, reflecting the fact that Beerbohm had referred to the 'heads' on the exterior of the hotel. In his novel, Beerbohm described them as being 'here in Oxford, exposed eternally and inexorably to wind and frost, to the four winds that lash them and the rains that wear them away, they are expiating, in effigy, the abomination of their pride and cruelty and lust. Who were lechers, they are without bodies, who were tyrants, they are crowned never but with crowns of snow, who made themselves even with the gods, they are by American visitors frequently mistaken for the Twelve Apostles.'

There are other literary links. The Alice Dining Room is decorated with scenes from *Alice in Wonderland* while in the film *Shadowlands*, C.S. Lewis is shown in the Fellows Lounge meeting Joy for the first time. While staying with friends at Holywell Mill, Dylan Thomas frequently lunched at the Randolph with his BBC colleagues.

Literary Links: Sir Max Beerbohm, Colin Dexter, Deborah Harkness, C.S. Lewis, Dylan Thomas

RIVER CHERWELL

The Cherwell, often known as the Isis in Oxford, rises in Northamptonshire and joins the River Thames on the southern edge of the city. The river runs through Summertown and past Lady Margaret Hall, Magdalen College, St Catherine's College, Wolfson College and the Dragon School.

The River Cherwell alongside Christ Church Meadow
(Bob Brewer, Wikimedia Commons/Creative Commons)

In *The Lord of the Rings*, Tolkien refers to the Withywindle River, complete with the character of Old Man Willow. It is believed that he took the idea for the river and Old Man Willow from the Cherwell that passed near his home. According to his son, John, Tolkien's drawing of Old Man River was based on an unpollarded willow on the river bank. A Tolkien memorial bench is sited beside the Cherwell.

The river has given its name to a local government district, and also to the university student newspaper, *Cherwell*.

Literary Links: Sir John Betjeman, Colin Dexter, Charles Dickens Jr, Philip Pullman, Ann Swinfen, J.R.R. Tolkien

RIVER ISIS

The name 'Isis' is used to describe the section of the River Cherwell, a tributary of the River Thames, as it flows through the city of Oxford. It has a long connection with the university since many of the colleges back onto the river, and rowing is one of the main sports enjoyed by students at the university. Numerous rowing regattas are held on the section of the river known as the Isis, such as the Christ Church Regatta and the Oxford University Regatta. Punting is another iconic water-based activity on this section of the river.

There are many literary links with the river as it flows through

The River Isis running through Oxford.
(Wikimedia Commons/Creative Commons)

Oxford and beyond. It was here that C.S. Lewis walked with his fellow Inklings J.R.R. Tolkien and Hugo Dyson discussing religion and mythology – a walk that led to the reawakening of C.S. Lewis's Christian faith.

Visitors to Oxford can walk in their footsteps along the river bank, following paths such as Addison's Walk.

Literary Links: Lewis Carroll, Val McDermid, C.S. Lewis, Percy Bysshe Shelley, J.R.R. Tolkien

SHELDONIAN THEATRE
Broad Street
Oxford
OX1 3AZ
www.sheldonian.ox.ac.uk

The theatre was designed by Sir Christopher Wren (Professor of Astronomy at Oxford) at an early point in his career when he was still gaining building and architectural experience. Inspired by Roman theatres, he used their D-shaped plan and in order to avoid using columns he devised

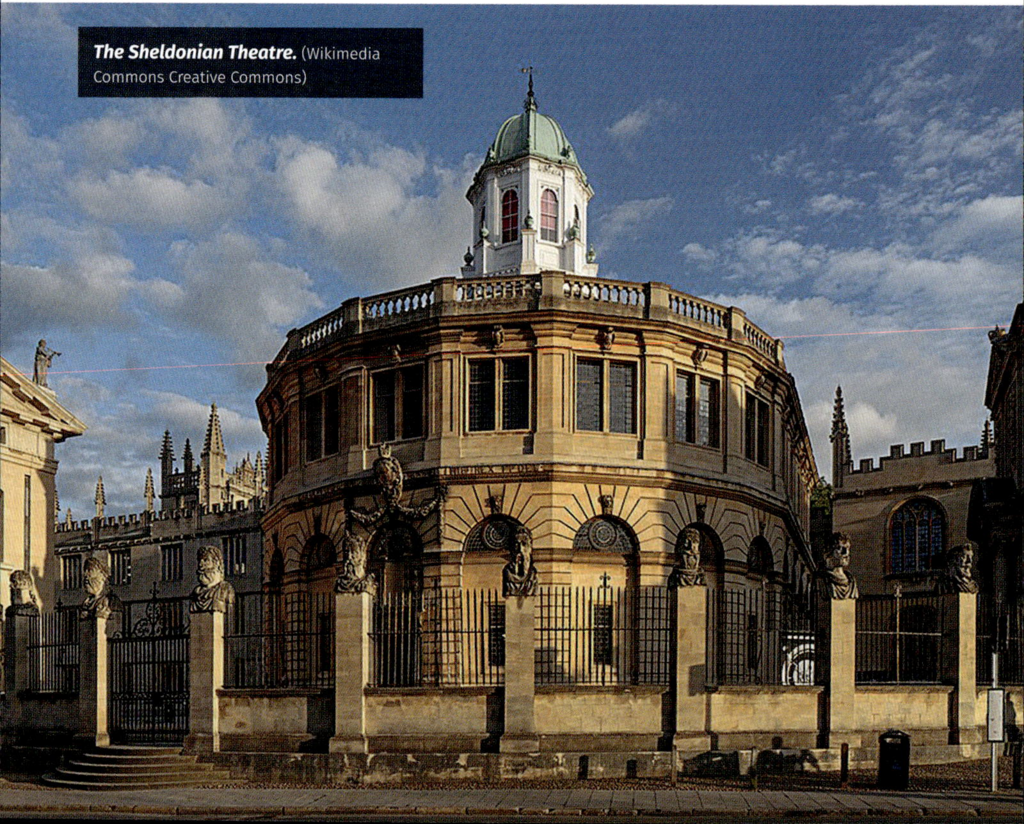

The Sheldonian Theatre. (Wikimedia Commons Creative Commons)

an innovative roof truss capable of spanning 21 metres. A baroque artwork by Robert Street adorns the roof, showing the triumph of Arts and Science over Envy, Rapine and Ignorance. It is now a Grade I listed building.

The Sheldonian is the main meeting place for the University of Oxford, particularly the congregation, which controls university affairs. All public ceremonies such as the granting of degrees are undertaken here and it would have been a familiar location to generations of Oxford graduates and dons such as C.S. Lewis and J.R.R. Tolkien.

In *Shadowlands*, Joy is filmed here during the singing of the national anthem, and it also features in Edmund Crispen's *The Moving Toyshop*.

The Sheldonian Theatre is open to the public whenever it is not required for events and university occasions. It may be closed at short notice. There is an entry change, allowing visitors access to the auditorium, old printing loft and cupola.

Literary Links: Edmund Crispin, Roald Dahl, Deborah Harkness, C.S. Lewis, Philip Pullman, J.K. Rowling

ST ALDATE'S POLICE STATION
St Aldate's
Oxford
OX1 1SZ

A plaque on the outside St Aldate's police station marks the site's links with the

St Aldate's police station, featured frequently in the* Inspector Morse *series (© David Hallam-Jones, Wikimedia Commons/Creative Commons/geograph.org.uk)

Inspector Morse Society. This exterior of the building was used to film scenes in the *Inspector Morse* series, starring John Thaw, between 1986 and 1995. Colin Dexter unveiled the plaque in 2006.

This is a working police station and is not open to the public. However, it has long been on the Morse tourist trail. Apparently before the plaque was installed, police officers experienced tourists coming to the station asking to speak to Inspector Morse.

Literary Links: Colin Dexter

ST ALDATE'S STREET
Oxford
OX1 1SR

Located in central Oxford, St Aldate's Street runs south from Carfax and many major buildings are located there, such as Christ Church, Pembroke College, Alice's Shop and the Museum of Oxford. It was once known as Fish Street, but is now called St Aldate's, reflecting the presence of St Aldate's church on the street. This is a street that would have been well known to Alice Liddell and her sisters, as well as Lewis Carroll.

St Aldate's Street appears on several occasions in *Morse*, *Lewis* and *Endeavour*. The police station was regularly used for filming.

Literary Links: Lewis Carroll, Colin Dexter

St Aldate's Street. (Wikimedia Commons/ Creative Commons/geograph.org.uk)

ST ALOYSIUS CHURCH

25 Woodstock Road
Oxford
OX2 6HA
www.oxfordoratory.org.uk

Founded by the Jesuits (Society of Jesus), this church was completed in 1875 and is located adjacent to Somerville College. It acted as the centre for Roman Catholic worship in Oxford. During the 1980s, it was taken over by the Archdiocese of Birmingham, and a new Oratorian community founded.

Gerald Manley Hopkins was among the many notable people linked to the church. A devout Catholic, J.R.R. Tolkien attended the church, and famously loved the Latin Mass said there.

Literary Links: Gerald Manley Hopkins, J.R.R. Tolkien

ST MARY MAGDALENE CHURCH

9 Magdalen St
Oxford
OX1 3AE
www.stmarymagdalenoxford.org.uk

An ancient parish church in central Oxford which follows the Anglo-Catholic tradition, St Mary Magdalene dates back to Saxon times. Having been rebuilt several times during the medieval period, it was restored between 1841 and 1842 by George Gilbert Scott, creating the first Gothic Revival interior in Oxford.

In the *Morse* episode 'Service of all the Dead', a series of murders set around St Frideswide's Church on the Cornmarket are said to have been inspired by the setting of St Mary Magdalen Church. The church has also appeared in *Lewis* and *Endeavour*.

Literary Links: Colin Dexter

ST MARY THE VIRGIN CHURCH

High Street
Oxford
OX1 4BJ
www.universitychurch.ox.ac.uk

▲ ***Church tower of St Mary the Virgin.*** (Bob Collowan, Wikimedia Commons/Creative Commons)

St Mary the Virgin has been a centre for worship for over 1,000 years. It was adopted by scholars and students of the university, and became its first building. By the early thirteenth century, it was being used for lectures and the awarding of degrees. In 1555, the church was the site of the trial of the Oxford Martyrs when Archbishop Cranmer, Bishop Latimer and Bishop Ridley were tried and found guilty of heresy. There is still a small section of Cranmer's Pillar within the church. John Wesley frequently worshipped here while studying in Oxford and later preached sermons while a fellow of Lincoln College. It was in this church that C.S. Lewis preached his sermon, 'The Weight of Glory'.

Literary Links: C.S. Lewis, John Wesley

ST MARY'S PASSAGE
High Street
Oxford
OX1 4BJ

St Mary's Passage is a small street leading off the High Street. It is well known for its 'Narnia Door', which belongs to a private house. The ornate door has a lion's head door knocker, and is flanked by two golden fawns. It is directly opposite the University Church of St Mary the Virgin. Close by is a lamp post and the combination of door and lamp post provided inspiration for an

▲ ***The Aslan Door, St Mary's Passage.*** (Wikimedia Commons/Creative Commons/Set in Stone Project)

early section in *The Lion, the Witch and the Wardrobe* by C.S. Lewis. He would have been very familiar with this site as he walked through the passage on many occasions while attending the adjacent church of St Mary.

Literary Links: C.S. Lewis

THE COVERED MARKET
High Street
Oxford
OX1 3DZ
www.oxford-coveredmarket.co.uk

There has been a covered market on this site since 1774 when the current building was constructed. It is reported that the building was created due to a desire to remove 'untidy, messy and unsavoury stalls' from the main streets of central Oxford. The architect was John Gwynn, who had already designed

▲ ***The Covered Market.*** (© Oxford City Council)

Magdalen Bridge. The Covered Market has entrances linking onto Market Street and High Street as well as access from the Cornmarket via Golden Cross Alley. Most of the market traders deal with different types of food, and there are cafés, bakeries and some butchers producing the classic Oxford sausage, as well as various gift shops. The Covered Market appears in many novels, for example *Jill* by Philip Larkin and Philip Pullman's *His Dark Materials*.

Literary Links: Deborah Harkness. Philip Larkin, Philip Pullman, Joanna Trollope

THE EAGLE AND CHILD PUB
49 St Giles' Street
Oxford
OX1 3LU

Sometimes known by its nickname the 'Bird and Baby', The Eagle and Child is located in St Giles'. In the seventeenth century it was owned by University College Oxford. In 2003, it was purchased by St John's College and has now been acquired by the Ellison Institute of Technology. The name The Eagle and Child was first used in 1684 and has been attributed to the legend of Ganymede, or to the crest of the Earl of Derby.

▲ ***Eagle and Child pub.*** (© Raymond Chapman/Wikimedia Commons/Geograph Britain & Ireland)

The Eagle and Child is most well known for its links with the Inklings literary group that included J.R.R. Tolkien, C.S. Lewis, Charles Williams and Hugo Dyson. The Inklings began meeting in C.S. Lewis's rooms at Magdalen College, which often led to informal gatherings in various Oxford pubs. Eventually, the group settled on The Eagle and Child, using a private lounge at the back of the pub known as the Rabbit Room. These meetings were usually held on Monday or Tuesday lunchtimes. The group met for a drink and discussed their work.

A sign above the fireplace contains a handwritten note to the landlord saying 'the undersigned, having just partaken of your ham, have drunk to your health', and is signed by members of the group.

The pub has appeared in various *Morse*, *Lewis* and *Endeavour* episodes.

Literary Links: Roger Lancelyn Green, C.S. Lewis, Deborah Harkness, The Inklings, J.R.R. Tolkien, Charles Williams

THE STORY MUSEUM
42 Pembroke Street
Oxford
OX1 1BP
www.storymuseum.org.uk

Dedicated to exploring stories of all kinds from ancient myths and legends to classic stories such as *Alice in Wonderland*, the museum contains a variety of displays and themed areas such as the Whispering Wood, City of Stories and Enchanted Library. There is also a theatre, a Hogwarts-inspired learning studio and an exhibition space. Younger children have their own themed area known as Small Worlds. Having initially operated as a virtual museum, it acquired premises of its own in 2009. The museum is located in a red brick building within walking distance of the Museum of Oxford, and was formerly a telephone exchange and pub.

There is a café on site. The museum is open daily and holds various events and special activities throughout the year.

Literary Links: Lewis Carroll, Cressida Cowell, Roald Dahl

▼ ***The Story Museum.*** (© John Cairns, The Story Museum)

TURF TAVERN
4 Bath Place
Oxford
OX1 3SU
www.greeneking.co.uk//turftavern

There has been a tavern on this site since 1381, and it is a popular venue with students, locals and visitors. A small building, the Turf Tavern is hidden at the end of a winding passage near the Bridge of Sighs, Hertford College and New College. This passage is narrow, and was once known as Hell Passage. Today it is called St Helen's Passage. In Evelyn Waugh's *Brideshead Revisited*, Charles Ryder remarks, 'The Turf in Hell Passage knew us well.' An alternative way to reach the pub is via the cobbled lane known as Bath Place.

According to historical records, the pub was once known as the Spotted Cow, but the name was later changed to the Turf Tavern. The tavern includes one of the few remaining sections of the original city wall. It still has a very distinct historic atmosphere when you walk in – the floors are uneven, small rooms are connected by narrow passageways, ceilings are low and there are lots of timber beams.

Among the many people who have frequented this pub are C.S. Lewis, J.R.R. Tolkien, Colin Dexter and the cast and crew of the *Harry Potter* films. It has appeared in numerous episodes of *Morse*, *Lewis* and *Endeavour* as a place where the central characters stop for a drink while discussing their latest case. Dylan Thomas often socialised at the Turf Tavern with friends and undergraduates while staying at Holywell Mill.

The pub is open daily, and is famous for its range of real ales as well as good basic food such as pies and fish and chips.

Literary Links: Colin Dexter, J.K. Rowling, Dylan Thomas, Evelyn Waugh

▲ ***Filming* Inspector Morse *at the Turf Tavern.***
(Wikimedia Commons/Creative Commons/Geograph.org.uk)

WESLEY MEMORIAL CHURCH
New Inn Hall Street
Oxford
OX1 2DH
www.wesleymem.org.uk

Built in 1878, the Wesley Memorial Church was designed by Charles Bell in a neo-Gothic style. It is where John and Charles Wesley began the Methodist movement. The first Methodist meeting house was created in Oxford in a rented room in New Inn Hall Street, where John Wesley first preached in 1783. Known as the Holy Club, it began as a group of students meeting to pray, study and show their faith through social outreach. From this small beginning, Methodism developed into a Church with over 70 million members around the world. A plaque on the wall at New Inn Hall Street marks that first sermon on 14 July 1783, when Wesley described the 'preaching house' as 'a lightsome, cheerful place'. A chapel was built further down the street in 1818, when it became the centre of the Oxford Wesleyan Methodist Circuit. As numbers grew, demand increased for a larger building leading to the creation of the Wesley Memorial Church.

The church possesses a significant amount of stained glass and is a memorial to John and Charles Wesley. It is open daily, with a programme of regular services and activities.

Literary Links: John and Charles Wesley

▲ ***Wesley Memorial Church.*** (© Wesley Memorial Church)

WHITE HORSE PUB
52 Broad Street
Oxford
OX1 3BB

Located in the centre of Oxford close to Blackwell's bookshop and the Sheldonian Theatre, this Grade II listed building dates back to the sixteenth century and is believed to be Oxford's smallest pub.

The White Horse was frequently used during the filming of *Inspector Morse*, *Lewis* and *Endeavour*. It is open daily, providing real ales and traditional home-cooked pub food.

Literary Links: Colin Dexter, Guillermo Martinez

OXFORD COLLEGES

ALL SOULS COLLEGE
High Street
Oxford
OX1 4AL
www.asc.ox.ac.uk

Founded by Henry VI in 1438 to commemorate the victims of the Hundred Years War, women were not admitted until 1978. Previous fellows include Sir Christopher Wren, T.E. Lawrence, and Cassandra Austen's maternal grandfather.

Unlike other colleges at Oxford University, All Souls has no student members. Instead, all members are fellows. Recent graduates from the university are able to apply for a small number of examination fellowships via competitive examination. It focuses very much on research. Deborah Harkness uses All Souls as a setting in her series *A Discovery of Witches*. The main character, Matthew Clairmont, is a fellow of the college, having written an essay on 'desire' in order to pass the entry examination in 1989.

Public access to the College Front, Great Quadrangle and chapel is available as individuals or in small groups free of charge during the afternoons and on Sundays. The college is closed to the public over Easter, Christmas and throughout August.

Literary Links: Jane Austen, Deborah Harkness, T.E. Lawrence

▲ ***All Souls College.*** (Bob Collowan, Wikimedia Commons/ Creative Commons)

BALLIOL COLLEGE
Broad St
Oxford
OX1 3BJ
www.balliol.ox.ac.uk

Balliol claims to be the oldest college in Oxford having operated on its current site since 1263. The story started three years earlier, when a dispute between John de Balliol and the Bishop of Durham became violent resulting in the bishop ordering Balliol to be whipped. Balliol was also ordered to pay a penance by renting a property and setting up a house of scholars. Following his death in 1269, John de Balliol's widow Dervoguilla of Galloway established a permanent endowment to establish Balliol College as the 'House of the Scholars of Balliol'.

The current building dates from the fifteenth century, together with buildings dating from the nineteenth century such as the chapel and Front Quad. The library contains extensive collections of early printed books and other archives, which can be accessed by the public. John Wycliffe, a master of Balliol, is credited with translating the Bible into English.

Balliol has many literary links including Graham Greene, the uncle of Cassandra Leigh, mother of Jane Austen, was President of Balliol. It also provided the inspiration for Dorothy L. Sayers's character Lord Peter Wimsey.

Balliol College. (Andrew Abbott, Wikimedia Commons/Creative Commons/Geograph Britain and Ireland)

The college is usually open to the public, on payment of an entry charge.

Literary Links: Matthew Arnold, Jane Austen, Hilaire Belloc, John Buchan, Graham Greene, Andrew Lang, Gerald Manley Hopkins, Dorothy L. Sayers, Algernon Swinburne

BRASENOSE COLLEGE
Radcliffe Square
Oxford
OX1 4AJ
www.bnc.ox.ac.uk

The college began as Brasenose Hall in the thirteenth century, and was eventually founded as a college in 1509. Many of the buildings such as the library and chapel were added in the seventeenth century, and a quadrangle over three centuries later. An unusual feature of the college is that it has a connecting door with Lincoln College which is only unlocked for five minutes every year, allowing a few Brasenose members to be served with ale by Lincoln College. Brasenose College Boat Club is one of the oldest rowing clubs in the world having been founded in 1815. Philip Pullman opened the newly renovated Greenland Library at the college in 2018.

▼ ***Brasenose College.*** (Wayland Smith, Wikimedia Commons/Creative Commons)

In 1793, Jane Austen accompanied by Cassandra Austen and their cousin Jane Cooper went to school in Oxford. Heading the school was the widow of the principal of Brasenose College, Mrs Anne Cawley. It was reported that Jane was not very happy at the school, especially after being given a sightseeing tour by her brother through 'dismal chapels, dusty libraries and greasy halls' resulting in her being given 'the vapours for two days afterwards'.

The college was used extensively during the filming of the Morse franchise, for example, in the *Inspector Morse* episode 'The Way Through the Woods'. On another occasion, Morse is a speaker at a university dinner set at Brasenose when a Japanese attendee is taken ill and later murdered, Morse is also shown talking to various academics in their college rooms or strolling through the grounds.

Visitors are able to access the college for a small donation, giving access to areas such as the Deer Park and the chapel. There is limited access to groups, which have to be pre-booked.

Literary Links: Jane Austen, Colin Dexter, James Gordon Farrell, William Golding, William Pater

CHRIST CHURCH
St Aldate's
Oxford
OX1 1DP
www.chch.ox.ac.uk

Originally this was designed to be Cardinal College, founded by Cardinal Thomas Wolsey on land previously used by St Frideswide's Priory. Following his

▼ ***Tom Tower, Christ Church.*** (Governing Body Christ Church Oxford, by permission)

fall from grace, the site was left empty until King Henry VIII set up Henry VIII's College in 1532. Further change came in 1546, when the king refounded it as Christ Church. It is the only college in the world that is also a cathedral. Christ Church has its own purpose-built Picture Gallery containing Old Master paintings and drawings.

Architecturally, the Great Quadrangle dates from Cardinal Wolsey's initiative, while other buildings have been added over the years such as Tom Tower, designed by Christopher Wren. Many of its buildings are Grade I listed, including the Hall, Chapter House and Christ Church Library.

Christ Church will forever be linked to one specific story – *Alice in Wonderland*. It was here that the Liddell sisters lived with their father, the Dean of Christ Church. Lewis Carroll was a mathematics tutor living-in across the quadrangle. There are many links with Alice Liddell, Lewis Carroll and *Alice in Wonderland*. A little door inside the cathedral garden is believed to be the inspiration for the door through which Alice entered Wonderland. Inside the college are features such as

▲ ***Christ Church Hall.*** (Governing Body Christ Church Oxford, by permission)

the *Alice in Wonderland* motifs in the large windows in the dining hall. In a fireplace are brass firedogs shaped like two ladies with long necks, which may have inspired the scene in which Alice tries the left-hand portion of a mushroom resulting in her neck growing extremely long.

Christ Church owns three collections of material linked to Lewis Carroll, including autographs, letters, manuscripts, original photographic prints, presentation copies and numerous translated editions of *Alice in Wonderland*, which are frequently used in special displays. Christ Church also has a collection of works by Edward Lear.

Apart from its links with *Alice*, Christ Church and its grounds have appeared in many films and TV series including *Harry Potter*, *The Golden Compass*, *X-Men*, *Morse*, *Lewis* and *Endeavour*. The grand staircase was used to film the famous entrance scene in which Professor McGonagall meets Harry Potter, Hermione and Ron for the first time while the Great Dining Hall inspired the Dining Hall at Hogwarts, recreated as a set in the studios. Other scenes filmed at Christ Church include Harry discovering the Quidditch trophy won by his father.

Christ Church has educated thirteen prime ministers, as well as King Edward VII and innumerable literary figures. It has incurred many literary references including W.B. Yeats's rhyme, in All Souls' Night:

Midnight has come and the great
Christ Church bell
And many a lesser bell sound
through the room;
And it is All Souls' Night.

Tickets to visit Christ Church can be pre-booked online, and are released on a weekly basis. These tickets offer a discounted entry price. Special guided tours can also be booked online. These tickets enable visitors to explore the college, cathedral and grounds, although an extra reduced charge is payable to enter the Picture Gallery.

Literary Links: Lewis Carroll, Michael Innes, John Masterman, Sir Thomas More, J.K. Rowling, John Ruskin, Dorothy L. Sayers, Sir Philip Sidney, Evelyn Waugh, John and Charles Wesley

CHRIST CHURCH CATHEDRAL
St Aldate's
Oxford
OX1 1DP
www.chch.ox.ac.uk

Christ Church is both the college chapel and the cathedral church for the Diocese of Oxford. The architecture includes Norman construction, medieval Gothic and remodelling in Victorian Gothic by Sir George Gilbert Scott during the nineteenth century. One of its most prominent features is a fifteenth-century stone

St Frideswide's Shrine, Christ Church Cathedral.
(Governing Body Christ Church Oxford, by permission)

vaulted chancel ceiling that has been described as one of the finest examples of its kind.

Construction began in the twelfth century and the church contains the shrine of St Frideswide, Oxford's patron saint. During the medieval period, the shrine was a popular pilgrim destination. Catherine of Aragon, Henry VIII's first queen, visited the shrine in the sixteenth century to pray for a son. The cathedral possesses some superb stained glass, particularly the Becket window dating back to 1320 making it a rare image of St Thomas à Becket to survive the Reformation. In the Latin Chapel, the St Frideswide Window was one of five windows designed by the pre-Raphaelite artist Edward Burne-Jones.

Religious services are held on a daily basis, with the Oxford Cathedral Choir participating on most occasions. Access for private prayer in the cathedral is possible via the Tom Gate entrance.

The cathedral has featured as a backdrop to many scenes in the *Harry Potter* films as well as in *Morse*, *Lewis* and *Endeavour*.

Guided tours are available, as well as special cathedral architecture and stained glass tours. Self-guided tickets are available on a daily basis. Pre-booking is recommended.

Literary Links: Lewis Carroll, Colin Dexter, Dorothy L. Sayers

CHRIST CHURCH GARDENS
St Aldate's
Oxford OX1 1DP
www.chch.ox.ac.uk/visit/gardens

The gardens surrounding Christ Church include extensive grass lawns in the Tom and Peckwater Quads, as well as the Cathedral Garden and Deanery Garden. The north wall of the Cathedral Garden contains 'Alice's Door' leading to the Deanery Garden. The Cloister Garden offers a quiet, contemplative area with lawns edged with lavender, an olive tree and a fountain. The Memorial Garden was designed as a permanent reminder of Christ Church students and staff who died in the Great War. It is inspired by the Arts and Crafts style complete with herbaceous borders and stone walls. Other gardens include the tree-lined Broad Walk, which would have been very familiar to Lewis Carroll and the Liddell sisters as it edges Christ Church Meadow.

Literary Links: Lewis Carroll

CHRIST CHURCH MEADOW
St Aldate's
Oxford
OX1 1DP
www.chch.ox.ac.uk/visit/meadow

A tranquil area in the centre of Oxford, Christ Church Meadow provides a place to relax, picnic, walk or run while enjoying views of the river,

▲ ***Christ Church Meadow.*** (Governing Body Christ Church Oxford, by permission)

Christ Church and the Oxford skyline. The meadow is Grade I listed. In 1783 James Sadler made the first British hot air balloon ascent from a site within the meadow. The fields are home to a herd of pedigree Old English Longhorn cattle.

Christ Church Meadow has always been a popular walking area, from which people embark to punt on the adjacent river. It was a filming location for the 1993 film *Shadowlands* – the story of C.S. Lewis and Joy Davidman.

Guided tours are periodically available from the head gardener, exploring conservation and planting schemes.

Entry to the meadow is free of charge. It is open to the public during daylight hours with the only exception being 25 December.

Literary Links: Lewis Carroll, C.S. Lewis, Philip Pullman

CLARENDON QUAD
Broad Street
Oxford
OX1 3AZ

Clarendon Quad forms part of the Bodleian Library complex, and is adjacent to Brasenose College. The Quad was constructed in the eighteenth century, taking its name from the Clarendon building on one side of the square which was the original home of Oxford University Press. Unlike other quadrangles in the colleges, Clarendon Quad is not a green space. Instead it is a large paved square used by people walking through Oxford or visiting the various surrounding buildings such as the Bodleian and Sheldonian Theatre.

The Quad was used in the filming of *Tinker, Tailor, Soldier, Spy* with Smiley seen to walk across it. It has also been used extensively when filming scenes for *Morse*, *Lewis* and *Endeavour*.

Access to Clarendon Quad is via Broad Street, Catte Street or Radcliffe Square.

Literary Links: John Le Carré, Colin Dexter

DEANERY, CHRIST CHURCH
Christ Church
St Aldate's
Oxford
OX1 1DP
www.chch.ox.ac.uk

The Dean of Christ Church acts as the head of the college as well as being Dean of Christ Church Cathedral, and lives in the Deanery building located in a corner of Tom Quad. Between 1855 and 1891, Henry Liddell was the dean. It was his daughter Alice who inspired the story of *Alice in Wonderland*. Lewis Carroll lived in college rooms overlooking the Dean's Garden where he saw the Liddell children playing. A friendship developed, with Carroll accompanying the Liddell children and their governess on walks and activities, and ultimately photographing them in various poses such as 'Alice the beggar child' in 1860.

There is no visitor access to the Deanery although pre-booked tickets can obtained to visit other buildings in Christ Church.

Literary Links: Lewis Carroll

CORPUS CHRISTI COLLEGE
Merton St
Oxford,
OX1 4JF
www.ccc.ox.ac.uk

Founded as a place of Renaissance learning by the Bishop of Winchester in 1517, Corpus Christi still contains elements of its Tudor origins. The Tudor portcullis and Catherine of Aragon's pomegranate emblem can be seen on the frieze inside the hall and on the chapel ceiling. Additional buildings were created during the eighteenth and nineteenth centuries. Among its members were Robert Bridges, Poet Laureate, and the art historian John Ruskin. The college was also closely involved with the translation of the Bible leading to the creation of the King James Bible.

One of its most notable architectural features is the Pelican

▲ ***Corpus Christi Front Quad.*** (© Corpus Christi)

▼ ***Corpus Christi garden.*** (© Corpus Christi)

Sundial. This is a large pillar dating from 1579, situated in the Front Quad. It gains its name from the gold-painted Pelican at the top of the pillar, with twenty-seven separate sundials located around the pillar.

An unusual feature of the college is the fact that it keeps at least one tortoise as a living mascot.

The college has been used as a filming location on many occasions especially with regard to *Morse*, *Lewis* and *Endeavour*.

Corpus Christi is open daily between 2.00 and 5.00 p.m., on request at the Porter's Lodge. There is no charge.

Literary Links: Colin Dexter, Vikram Seth

EXETER COLLEGE
Turl Street
Oxford
OX1 3DP
www.exeter.ox.ac.uk

This site has been occupied by Exeter College since 1315. By the seventeenth century, it had become one of the leading Oxford colleges resulting in the construction of a new hall and chapel. Among its graduates are Pre-Raphaelite leaders William Morris and Edward Burne-Jones. There are major works by them on view in the Morris Room and the chapel. In 2014, J.K. Rowling was elected an honorary fellow due to the 'extraordinary contribution she has made to the field of literature, and in particular to children's reading and literacy'.

Exeter College has several other literary links. J.R.R. Tolkien studied here, during which time he began to formulate his ideas about Middle Earth. He graduated in 1915 with first-class honours. Tolkien was awarded the Skeat Prize for English and the college library now owns the book presented to him on winning that prize. Exeter College also acted as the inspiration for Philip Pullman's Jordan College in the *His Dark Materials* trilogy, and was used for location filming of *The Golden Compass*. It has also appeared in episodes of *Morse*, *Lewis* and *Endeavour*, particularly 'The Remorseful Day' where Morse suffers a heart attack while in the college. Exeter

▲ ***Exeter College chapel.*** (Diliff, Wikimedia Commons/Creative Commons)

College appeared in the filming of Vera Brittain's *Testament of Youth*.

Public access to the college is available between 2 and 5 p.m. daily. There is a charge payable.

Literary Links: Alan Bennett, Vera Brittain, Colin Dexter, Deborah Harkness, William Morris, Philip Pullman, J.R.R. Tolkien

HERTFORD COLLEGE
Catte Street
Oxford
OX1 3BW
www.hertford.ox.ac.uk

The college was originally founded in the 1280s as Hart Hall, but was dissolved in 1816. The site was taken over by Magdalen Hall, which eventually became Hertford College. By far the most distinctive aspect of Hertford is its iconic Bridge of Sighs linking the Old and New Quadrangles. This bridge has been used as a filming location on countless occasions.

Prominent authors linked to Hertford include Evelyn Waugh, John Donne and Jonathan Swift. Recalling his time at Hertford, Waugh wrote 'I do no work here and never got to Chapel.' Apparently he had an ongoing feud

▲ ***Hertford College.*** (Simononly/Wikipedia Media/Creative Commons)

with his history tutor at Hertford, and later used him as a basis for various unpleasant characters in his novels.

Hertford College is closed to tourists.

Literary Links: John Donne. Jonathan Swift, Evelyn Waugh

JESUS COLLEGE
Turl Street
Oxford
OX1 3DW
www.jesus.ox.ac.uk

Jesus College was the only college to be founded during the reign of Elizabeth I. Initially it was wholly Welsh, having been founded specifically for the education of Welsh students, mainly clergy. A close link with Wales has been maintained, and the college still attracts many Welsh students. Work on the quadrangles began during the seventeenth century. Over the centuries, the scope of subjects studied at Jesus expanded significantly. One of its most well known students was T.E. Lawrence, who studied history there and developed his abiding interest in the Middle East, researching a thesis on crusader castles.

Public access to the college is possible during the afternoons in the

▲ ***Jesus College.*** (Kaihsu, Wikimedia Commons/Creative Commons)

form of pre-booked organised tours, and a charge is payable.

Literary Links: T.E. Lawrence

KEBLE COLLEGE
Parks Road
Oxford
OX1 3PG
www.keble.ox.ac.uk

One of the largest colleges in Oxford, Keble was founded in 1870 as a memorial to John Keble, a leading member of the Oxford Movement, which sought to restore the Catholic heritage of the Church of England. The college is no longer linked to the Anglican Church, with students studying the full range of academic disciplines. C.S. Lewis stayed here while training as an officer cadet following his call-up into the army in 1917. His unit was stationed at Keble. He wrote that he was living in a 'carpetless little cell with two beds (minus sheets or pillows)'. Of the five young men who trained with him as officer cadets at Keble, Lewis was the only one who survived the carnage of the battlefield.

Keble College has a distinctive appearance as it is built in a Victorian

▲ ***Keble College from across Liddon Quad.*** (Shiva, Wikimedia Commons/Creative Commons)

Gothic red brick style. Unlike other colleges, the rooms are arranged along corridors rather than staircases. It is mentioned in John Betjeman's poem 'Myfanwy at Oxford'. Keble College side chapel houses the original of William Holman Hunt's painting *The Light of the World*.

The college was used for the filming of *Endeavour* when the young Morse was investigating the murder of a don. For the purposes of filming, it became Baidley College and was covered in snow. Author Deborah Harkness studied at Keble, and her memories of those days are reflected in the descriptions of academic life in her book *A Discovery of Witches*.

Keble College is open to the public between 2 and 5 p.m. daily, and there is no charge. Contact the Porter's Lodge for admittance.

Literary Links: Cressida Cowell, Colin Dexter, Deborah Harkness

LADY MARGARET HALL
Norham Gardens
Oxford
OX2 6QA
www.lmh.ox.ac.uk

Founded in 1878 and named after Lady Margaret Beaufort, the mother of King Henry VII, Lady Margaret Hall was one of the first women's colleges at Oxford,

▲ ***Lady Margaret Hall.*** (Philip Halling, Wikimedia Commons/Creative Commons)

providing women with a degree-level education. This pioneering aspect of its role has been maintained over the years as it is now the only Oxford college to offer a foundation year at lower entrance requirements for students from minority and under-represented backgrounds so as to prepare them for an undergraduate degree.

The college backs onto the River Cherwell, with its first building being located on Norham Gardens. Subsequent buildings steadily took the college down to the river, before moving back towards Norham Gardens via a series of quadrangles.

There are many literary links here. In 1919, Tolkien provided private tuition to many Lady Margaret Hall students. His daughter, Priscilla, attended the college, graduating in 1951.

Harper Lee, author of *To Kill a Mockingbird*, was a visiting student. Antonia Fraser was also a student at Lady Margaret.

Iris Murdoch used to enjoy walking through the gardens of Lady Margaret Hall. A memorial bench named in her honour can now be found there.

Lady Margaret Hall has provided the inspiration for many fictional colleges. In Philip Pullman's

The Secret Commonwealth, Lyra Belacqua attends an Oxford college modelled on lady Margaret Hall, while in *Fire and Hemlock*, Dianna Wynne Jones refers to St Margaret's College. Val McDermid's novel *Trick of the Dark* deals with St Scholastika's college, which has grounds backing onto the river and buildings made from red and yellow brick.

Visitors are welcome and are not charged for entry.

Literary Links: Antonia Fraser, Harper Lee, Val McDermid, Iris Murdoch, Philip Pullman, J.R.R. Tolkien, Dianna Wynne Jones

LINCOLN COLLEGE
Turl Street
Oxford
OX1 3DR
www.lincoln.ox.ac.uk

Founded by Richard Fleming, Bishop of Lincoln, in 1427 with the aim of combatting John Wycliffe and the Lollards, Lincoln College has grown steadily. In the eighteenth century, it became the centre of Methodism when John and Charles Wesley established a 'Holy Club'. John Wesley later signed himself as 'John Wesley, sometime fellow of Lincoln College'. There is a portrait of Wesley inside

▼ ***Lincoln College.*** (Christine Matthews, Wikimedia Commons/Creative Commons

the college as well as a bust in the front quadrangle.

A variety of literary works have been set at Lincoln College such as the historical crime novel, *Heresy*, by S.J. Parris. It has also been used for filming episodes of *Morse*, *Lewis* and *Endeavour*.

Literary Links: John Le Carré, Colin Dexter, S.J. Parris, Dr Seuss, Veronica Stallwood, John and Charles Wesley

MAGDALEN COLLEGE
High Street
Oxford
OX1 4AU
www.magd.ox.ac.uk

Magdalen was founded in 1458 by the Lord Chancellor, William Waynflete, Bishop of Winchester. It soon became one of the most prominent colleges in Oxford, with students such as Thomas Wolsey, later chief adviser to Henry VIII. Architecturally the college is arranged around five quadrangles, composed of buildings from the medieval period to the nineteenth century. Two of the most stunning buildings are the Founders Tower, built in medieval High Gothic style complete with pinnacles, carvings and bosses, and the Great Tower (Magdalen Tower), which has become an iconic Oxford landmark, providing inspiration for other towers worldwide including the Mitchell Tower at the University of Chicago. It was built between 1492 and 1509, and contains a peal of bells, which are regularly rung. The tower forms the centre of May Day celebrations involving the Magdalen choir singing from the top of the tower while the Dean of Magdalen pronounces a blessing.

The college grounds include a pretty water meadow as well as Addison's Walk, a tree-lined path that was used by J.R.R. Tolkien and C.S. Lewis.

Magdalen College was the home of C.S. Lewis for many years and provided much inspiration. In the cloisters, there

are numerous carvings of animals on the pillars which give the impression that Aslan, the great lion, is about to breathe on them and bring them to life. The Inklings read their latest works to each other at Lewis's rooms at the college, and the film *Shadowlands* starts with a service in Magdalen chapel before progressing to a formal meal in the dining room. Joy and C.S. Lewis are also shown watching the May Day festivities and listening to the choir on the Great Tower.

There are many other literary links including Alan Garner and Sir John Betjeman, while an entire room is devoted to Oscar Wilde with a frieze focusing on his works.

Visitor access to Magdalen is via the Porter's Lodge. The college is open daily from 10 a.m., unless closed for college events. There is an admission charge. During the summer season, guided tours are provided twice a day.

Literary Links: Sir John Betjeman, Alan Garner, T.E. Lawrence, C.S. Lewis, Compton Mackenzie, Oscar Wilde

Magdalen College. (© Magdalen College)

MERTON COLLEGE
Merton Street
Oxford
OX1 4JD
www.merton.ox.ac.uk

Merton College was the first completely self-governing college at Oxford University, and it is claimed that the college's Mob Library is also the oldest continuously functioning university library. During the medieval period, all the library books were stored in locked chests and could only be borrowed by academic staff. Some of the books were so special that they were chained to the desks.

The college was founded in 1264 by Walter de Merton, and built in three phases between 1288 and 1378. Architecturally, additional works were undertaken in the seventeenth and nineteenth centuries.

An unusual quirk of the college is its October Quad walk, in which students walk backwards around the quadrangle while wearing full academic dress. Also known as the Time Ceremony, it marks the change from British Summer Time to Greenwich Mean Time and lasts a full hour. The students link arms creating long chains of people and spin at each corner of the quad.

Among its former students and academics are Tolkien, Max Beerbohm, Andrew Lang and T.S. Elliot. A lecture theatre was named in honour of Eliot in 2010.

Merton College. (Jonas Magnus Lystad, Wikimedia Commons/Creative Commons)

Not surprisingly, various episodes of *Morse*, *Lewis* and *Endeavour* were filmed here. The college also features in 'Queen Charlotte', a Bridgerton Story based on Julia Quinn's Regency-style romance novels.

Merton College is open daily between 2 and 5 p.m. unless there is a college event. Access is via the Porter's Lodge. An entry charge is payable. Visitors are welcome to attend chapel services.

Literary Links: Max Beerbohm, Colin Dexter, T.S. Eliot, Mark Haddon, Roger Lancelyn Green, Andrew Lang, Guillermo Martinez, Ann Swinfen, J.R.R. Tolkien

NEW COLLEGE
Holywell Street
Oxford
OX1 3BN
www.new.ox.ac.uk

When founded in 1379, the college was known as The College of St Mary of Winchester in Oxford, reflecting the role of its founder, William of Wykeham as Bishop of Winchester. This caused confusion with Oriel College, also dedicated to the Virgin Mary. As a result, the college soon became known as New College. An innovative approach to architectural design was adopted for the college, since all the buildings were based around an enclosed quadrangle thus giving easy access to accommodation, chapel, library and dining hall. In due course, other colleges adopted a similar concept.

During the English Civil War, the college warden helped to organise the defence of New College, and Oxford generally, in support of the king. After the Royalist defeat, the Parliamentarian Lord Saye, who had studied at the College, promptly imprisoned the warden.

A major development came in the early seventeenth century when New College needed more accommodation for its students. Instead of building a traditional quadrangle, it introduced the Garden Quad, a three-sided design reportedly modelled on the Palace of Versailles. This Garden Quad leads to gardens encircled by thirteenth-century city walls containing colourful herbaceous borders and an ornamental mound.

Among the stunning buildings are the peaceful cloisters famous for the Holm oak featured in *Harry Potter and the Goblet of Fire*. The original Front Quad was devised by William of Wykeham, while the dining hall is the oldest and tallest of its kind. Artworks on display include Jacob Epstein's statue of Lazarus located in the ante-chapel. On Longwall Street, the college premises include the Morris Garages, a historic site where William Richard Morris pioneered the production of motor cars.

Tourist access is via the entrance on New College Lane, and there is an admission charge. Opening hours vary

▲ ***New College cloisters.*** (Simon Q, Wikimedia Commons/Creative Commons)

according to the season, with winter opening hours limited primarily to the afternoons. A printed guide is provided to enable visitors to explore the college as they wish.

Literary Links: Colin Dexter, John Fowles, John Galsworthy, Deborah Harkness, Philip Pullman, J.K. Rowling

ORIEL COLLEGE
Oriel Square
Oxford
OX1 4EW
www.oriel.ox.ac.uk

Originally known as the College of the Blessed Virgin Mary, Oriel gained its name from a donated property known as La Oriole, located on what is now the Front Quadrangle. The college grew slowly over the years, and began teaching undergraduates in the early 1500s. George Washington numbers among its famous alumni. Later Oriel became an active member of the Oxford Movement religious revival, involving academics like Dr Thomas Arnold and John Henry Newman.

Oriel College and grounds are instantly recognisable to followers

▲ ***Oriel College.*** (Creative Commons)

of *Morse*, *Lewis* and *Endeavour* since they were used extensively for filming episodes such as 'The Daughters of Cain' (*Morse*), 'Magnus Opus' (*Lewis*) and 'Arcadia' (*Endeavour*).

The college is usually open to visitors between 2 and 5 p.m. daily. Access is via the Porter's Lodge on Oriel Square, where entrance fees are payable.

Literary Links: Mathew Arnold, Colin Dexter, Thomas Hughes, Michael Innes, Sir Thomas More

PEMBROKE COLLEGE
St Aldate's
Oxford
OX1 1DW
www.pmb.ox.ac.uk

The college was founded in 1624 by King James I, on land formerly used by a college hostel known as Broadgates Hall. It was named in honour of William Herbert, Earl of Pembroke, Chancellor of the University of Oxford. By far the most well known member of the college is J.R.R. Tolkien who was a fellow for twenty years during which he wrote his

▲ ***Chapel Quad, Pembroke College.*** (Wikimedia Commons/Creative Commons)

most famous stories *The Hobbit* and *The Lord of the Rings*.

Pembroke College is not regularly open to members of the public. It occasionally allows visits with prior arrangement via the Lodge.

Literary Links: Colin Dexter, Samuel Johnson, Thomas Lovell Beddoes, J.R.R. Tolkien

RUSKIN SCHOOL OF ART

The Old Music Hall
108 Cowley Road, entrance 54 Marston Street
Oxford
OX4 1JE
www.rsa.ox.ac.uk

Set up by Victorian art critic and writer John Ruskin in 1871 and equipped with extensive resources such as over 400 artworks and prints by leading masters like Durer, Tintoretto and Turner, the school was originally based in the Ashmolean Museum of Art and Archaeology with the aim of eventually setting up a degree-level course in art. That particular aim took much longer than anticipated with the first undergraduate degrees in fine arts not being awarded until 1981 by which time the school had moved to its existing site.

Literary Links: John Ruskin

SOMERVILLE COLLEGE
Woodstock Road
Oxford
OX2 6HD
www.some.ox.ac.uk

Founded in 1879, Somerville was one of the first colleges established to provide a university education for women. It was named after Mary Somerville, a Scottish mathematician and scientific writer, who believed that women should have equal access to education as well as the right to vote. Somerville students quickly showed that they were capable of high academic achievement and the college gained its charter in 1926, five years after women were finally granted degrees. Somerville was active in the women's suffrage campaign prior to the First World War. Its library is said to be one of the largest in the university. The first male students were admitted in 1994.

Somerville has attracted many writers over the years, such as Vera Brittain, Susan Cooper and Iris Murdoch. It provided the inspiration for Dorothy L. Sayers's novel *Gaudy Night*.

During term time, Somerville is usually open to the public on a daily basis but it is recommended that potential visitors should check access before visiting.

Literary Links: Vera Brittain, Susan Cooper, Rose Maculay, Faith Martin, Iris Murdoch, Dorothy L. Sayers, Ann Swinfen, Siegfried Sassoon

▼ ***Somerville College.*** (Philip Allfrey, Wikimedia Commons/Creative Commons)

ST ANNE'S COLLEGE
56 Woodstock Road
Oxford
OX2 6HS
www.st-annes.ox.ac.uk

St Anne's was set up by a group of radical Victorians who believed there should be a way for women to study without being part of a college. Operated by the Society of Home-Students, women were allowed to live in lodgings anywhere in the city, attending lectures and seminars in order to provide a more affordable way of gaining a degree-level education. The only shared space was located outside the principal's living room. It was not until 1937 that the society acquired a permanent home in Woodstock Road. In 1942, there was a name change to St Anne's Society so as to reflect the new premises. By 1959, it had acquired full college status and continued to expand over succeeding decades, adding accommodation blocks and teaching buildings.

Among its well-known graduates are Helen Fielding, author of the ever popular *Bridget Jones's Diary*, while Iris Murdoch was a fellow at the college, teaching philosophy.

The college welcomes visitors on a daily basis between 9 and 5 p.m. to explore its grounds. Access is free but donations are welcomed.

Literary Links: Helen Fielding, Penelope Lively, Iris Murdoch

St Anne's College. (© St Anne's College)

ST CROSS COLLEGE
61 St Giles'
Oxford OX1 3LX
www.stx.ox.ac.uk

A purely graduate college focusing on research, St Cross was founded in 1965 and is named for the street in which its first building was located. It moved to its existing site in St Giles' in 1981, taking over the Gothic style Pusey House linked to the Oxford Movement. A new south wing was built in the 1990s providing more facilities and student accommodation.

In 2005, Colin Dexter was elected a fellow of the college, reflecting the importance and popularity of his Inspector Morse books.

St Cross College is not open to the general public, although it often participates in the 'Oxford Open Doors' scheme held during September every year.

Literary Links: Colin Dexter

ST HILDA'S COLLEGE
Cowley Place
Oxford
OX4 1DY
www.st-hildas.ox.ac.uk

Named after the Anglo-Saxon Saint Hilda of Whitby, the college was founded in 1883 as a women's hall, obtaining a royal charter as St Hilda's College in 1926. Located at the end of the High Street,

St Cross College. (Kaihsu Tai, Wikimedia Commons/Creative Commons)

St Hilda's College. (Vieve Forward/Wikimedia Commons/Creative Commons)

just over Magdalen Bridge, the site has six major buildings. Its grounds stretch along the banks of the River Cherwell, and it has its own fleet of punts. Until 2008, St Hilda's was purely female.

The first principal of St Hilda's was Dorothea Beale, a suffragist and educational reformer who wrote extensively about female education. Among the many authors who are former students at St Hilda's are Susanna Clarke, Barbara Pym, Daisy Dunn, D.K. Broster and Val McDermid. It is well known for its annual Crime Fiction Weekend. Val McDermid has used St Hilda's as inspiration for locations in her novels.

Visitor access is by appointment only. There is no charge.

Literary Links: Susanna Clarke, Val McDermid, Barbara Pym

ST HUGH'S COLLEGE
St Margaret's Road
Oxford
OX2 6LE
www.st-hughs.ox.ac.uk

Another women's hall set up in late Victorian times with the aim of opening up Oxford education to poorer women, since its foundation in 1886 by Elizabeth Wordsworth, grand-niece of poet William Wordsworth, the college has played a major role in women's education. During the Second World War, it was turned into a hospital for military personnel suffering from head injuries. Male undergraduates were admitted for the first time in 1987.

▲ ***St Hugh's College.*** (Nigel Cox Wikimedia Commons/ Creative Commons)

The college has been used as a backdrop for filming the *Endeavour* series.

St Hugh's welcomes visitors, but asks that people check opening times in advance. There is no charge.

Literary Links: Colin Dexter, Philip Larkin, Joanna Trollope

ST JOHN'S COLLEGE
St Giles'
Oxford
OX1 3JP
www.sjc.ox.ac.uk

The college began life as a centre for Cistercian monks studying at Oxford University in 1437. After the dissolution of the monasteries in 1536, the land and buildings went to the king who granted them to his new college, Christ Church. In 1555, the site was acquired by Sir Thomas White, a wealthy London merchant and member of the powerful Merchant Taylors' Company who founded a new educational institution known as the College of St John the Baptist. The link remained until the nineteenth century.

Over the years St John's College has become closely linked with literature. During the late eighteenth and early nineteenth centuries, Jane Austen's father and brothers attended the college. Other graduates have included A.E. Houseman, Kingsley Amis, Philip Larkin and Edmund Crispin. It has also

▲ **St John's College.** (Wikimedia Commons/Creative Commons)

featured as a location in *Morse*, *Lewis* and *Endeavour*.

Visitors are welcome to explore the gardens, Front Quad, Canterbury Quad, the chapel and the Kendrew Quad free of charge. Opening hours are generally during the afternoon.

Literary Links: Kingsley Amis, Jane Austen, Edmund Crispin, Colin Dexter, Robert Graves, A.E. Housman, Philip Larkin

THE QUEEN'S COLLEGE
High Street
Oxford OX1 4AW
www.queens.ox.ac.uk

Dating from 1341, The Queen's College was named in honour of Philippa of Hainault, Queen of England

The Queen's College. (Robin Sones, Wikimedia Commons/Creative Commons/Geograph Britain and Ireland)

and wife to Edward III. Built in a neoclassical style, the college's Front Quad appeared as a major landmark on the Queen Elizabeth II Diamond Jubilee commemorative stamps. Its library contains several distinctive elements such as the seventeenth-century highly decorated ornamental white plasterwork ceiling, as well as two eighteenth-century papier mâché globes.

The college was used for filming scenes in the *Inspector Morse* and *Endeavour* series.

Literary Links: Colin Dexter, Walter Pater

TRINITY COLLEGE
Broad Street
Oxford
OX1 3BH
www.trinity.ox.ac.uk

Initially, Trinity was founded as a training house for Catholic priests. From the seventeenth century onwards there has been considerable rivalry between Trinity and Balliol Colleges, especially on the sports field and river. This rivalry is reflected in Dorothy L. Sayers's novel, *Five Red Herrings*, in which Lord Peter Wimsey is asked if he remembers a Trinity contemporary. He answers, 'I never knew any Trinity men. The Jews have no dealings with the Samaritans.'

Trinity College buildings date mainly from the seventeenth century, while its chapel was the first to be designed entirely in the baroque style.

Trinity was one of the locations used for filming episodes of *Inspector Morse*, *Lewis* and *Endeavour* as well as *Brideshead Revised*.

At weekends, visitors are welcome to explore the gardens, Main Quad and

▲ ***Trinity College.*** (Emma White Wikimedia Commons/Creative Commons)

chapel. Opening hours are variable depending on whether any private college events are being held. Access is via the Porter's Lodge.

Literary Links: Colin Dexter, Sir Arthur Quiller-Couch, Simon Tolkien

UNIVERSITY COLLEGE
High Street
Oxford OX1 4BH
www.univ.ox.ac.uk

One of the oldest colleges in Oxford, University College was founded in 1249 by William of Durham. One of its distinctive features is the Logic Lane covered bridge, which links two sides of the college. The eastern side is primarily student accommodation while the western side is used as a library, chapel, college offices and more accommodation around the quadrangles. One of the more unusual buildings is the Shelley Memorial depicting Percy Bysshe Shelley dead on a seashore in Italy. This well-known Romantic poet was sent down from the college after writing *The Necessity of Atheism*.

▲ ***University College Hall.*** (© University College Oxford)

Radcliffe Tower. (© University College Oxford)

The college's most well-known student is C.S. Lewis, who gained a scholarship to University College and came up to Oxford in 1917. After a gap due to war service, Lewis returned to University College and obtained a double-first in greats, followed by a first in English. As a student his rooms overlooked the Radcliffe Quad.

The college is currently closed to visitors except during university open days and 'Oxford Open Doors' each September.

Literary Links: C.S. Lewis, Ian Morson, V.S. Naipaul, Percy Bysshe Shelley, Sir Stephen Spender

WADHAM COLLEGE
Parks Road
Oxford
OX1 3PN
www.wadham.ox.ac.uk

When Nicholas Wadham died in 1609 he left his fortune to endow a college at Oxford. His widow Dorothy assumed the task of fulfilling his wishes by obtaining a site, dealing with the administration and fighting off relatives who opposed the will. Within four years, the college was up and running. It became particularly well known for its scientific interests, and in the seventeenth century was the meeting place for the astronomers, anatomists

Wadham College. (Lewis Clarke, Wikimedia Commons/Creative Commons/geography.org)

and chemists who eventually formed the Royal Society. Sir Christopher Wren studied there and Poet Laureate Cecil Day-Lewis joined the college in 1923. Other literary alumni include author and broadcaster Melvyn Bragg.

Architecturally, Wadham is an example of Jacobean Gothic, with its front quadrangle acting as the entire college building for many years. It's hall and chapel are built in Jacobean style with wooden panelling and hammer beam roofs. The extensive gardens contain a notable collection of trees including 'Tree of Heaven', a rare Chinese gutta-percha, ginkgo, giant redwood and a tulip tree.

Wadham College is open in the afternoons during term time, and for longer periods during holidays. There is no charge for entry.

Literary Links: Melvyn Bragg, Cecil Day-Lewis

WORCESTER COLLEGE
Walton St
Oxford
OX1 2HB
www.worc.ox.ac.uk

There has been a college on this site since the thirteenth century when it was known as Gloucester College.

Worcester College. (© Worcester College)

Reminders of that history can still be seen above the entrance to staircase 10, which is marked with the arms of Gloucester College. Its fortunes declined during the sixteenth and seventeenth centuries, resulting in the college folding at the beginning of the eighteenth century. Following the injection of funds from Worcestershire baronet Sir Thomas Cookes, Gloucester College was refounded as Worcester College. Rebuilding work began and included a new library. The grounds are extensive with gardens and an arboretum. The college has been used as a location for *Morse*, *Lewis* and *Endeavour*.

Visitors are welcome to explore the gardens of Worcester College during the afternoons during term time. Longer opening hours are possible during holiday periods.

Literary Links: Colin Dexter, John Masterman, Thomas de Quincey

OUTER OXFORD

AMPLEFORTH ARMS PUB
53 Collingwood Road
Headington
Oxford
OX3 8HH
www.amplefortharms.co.uk

Built by Ind Coope in 1939 to cater for a newly-built housing estate, C.S. Lewis frequently went to the Ampleforth for a drink accompanied by his brother Warnie and J.R.R. Tolkien. Local people who saw them at the time are reported to have commented that they 'were often engrossed in conversation that was way above the heads of us locals'. On 15 December 1958, Lewis wrote of a visit to the pub with his wife Joy saying, 'She walks (with a stick and a limp) about the wood shooting – or anyway shooting at – pigeons; we walk together to the Ampleforth Arms.'

The pub closed in 2014 but remained under the ownership of Punch Taverns. Traditionally a pub focused on drinking beer, it was taken over in 2023 by Soulfood Spices Ltd with the aim of providing a food offer to patrons.

Related locations nearby include Headington, Holy Trinity Church, The Kilns, 10 Old High Street, C.S. Lewis Nature Reserve, Sandfield Road and St Andrews Church.

Literary Links: C.S. Lewis, J.R.R. Tolkien

BOARS HILL
Oxford
OX1 5HR

Located on the outskirts of Oxford, Boars Hill is a sloping woodland area, offering superb views across Oxford. On Foxcombe Road, the St Thomas More Chapel attracts attention. A small chapel, it was a tiny garage during the Second World War. Following growing demand from Catholics in the area, the garage was converted to a chapel dedicated to St Thomas More, a one-time student at Oxford.

The chapel and Boars Hill are well known to students, especially poets. Matthew Arnold strolled its slopes with his friend Arthur Hugh Clough, and coined the phrase 'dreaming spires' for Oxford. Other famous literary people visiting Boars Hill have included Robert Bridges and John Masefield. Robert Graves lived in a cottage with his wife, Nancy Richardson, in a house rented from John Masefield. Nancy started a small grocer's shop in the village but it collapsed after six months due mainly to opposition from Mrs Masefield, who disliked the number of tourists it attracted. This led Robert Graves and Nancy Richardson to move to Islip.

Evelyn Waugh's *Brideshead Revisited* includes the sentence, 'advice from a fourth year man ... Keep clear of Boars Hill'.

▲ ***View from Boars Hill. Christopher.*** (Hilton Georgraph.org.uk Wikimedia commons)

Literary Links: Robert Graves, John Masefield, Sir Thomas More, Evelyn Waugh

C.S. LEWIS NATURE RESERVE
5 Lewis Close
Headington
Oxford
OX3 8JD
www.bbowt.org.uk/naturereserves/cslewis

Managed by the Berkshire, Buckinghamshire and Oxfordshire Wildlife Trusts, the reserve is located on land formerly owned by C.S. Lewis behind his house, The Kilns. Occupying three hectares of tranquil woodland containing mainly beech, ash, oak, birch, alder and hawthorn trees, it is a setting that was very familiar to Lewis. He loved nature, and this wooded area was one of the features that attracted him to the house. It provided inspiration for him when creating the Narnian landscape. Lewis added many more trees to the woodland, along with paths and seats. Visitors to the nature reserve can walk the same paths, see the flooded clay pit lake and the trees he planted.

Entry to the reserve is free and it is open day and night throughout the year.

▲ ***C.S. Lewis Nature Reserve.*** (Steve Daniels, Wikimedia Commons/Creative Commons/Geograph.org.uk)

Related locations are the Ampleforth Arms, Headington, Holy Trinity Church, The Kilns and 10 Old High Street.

Literary Links: C.S. Lewis

DRAGON SCHOOL
Bardwell Road
Oxford
OX2 6SS
www.dragonschool.org

Numerous literary names began their education at the Dragon School including Sir John Betjeman, Antonia Fraser and William Fiennes. It is a co-educational private school founded in 1877 by a group of Oxford dons. Initially teaching took place in rooms within Balliol Hall, but its popularity led the school to move to a standalone site. In 1894, the Dragon School erected new buildings on its current site at Bardwell, North Oxford. Initially the school was known as Oxford Preparatory School but over time the name 'Dragon' was adopted. It is a popular, independent, day and boarding school.

Among the children educated here was Humphrey Carpenter, who later wrote about C.S. Lewis and the Inklings. Other students have included Sir John Betjeman and Antonia Fraser.

The school is not open to the public.

Literary Links: Sir John Betjeman, Antonia Fraser, William Fiennes, Simon Tolkien

THE HARCOURT ARMS PUB
Cranham
Jericho
Oxford
OX2 6DG
www.harcourtarmsjericho.co.uk

There has been a pub on this site since 1869, but the current building dates from 1938. It was named after the wealthy Harcourt family who lived in Nuneham Courtney. Sir William Harcourt was an Oxford MP between 1869 and 1880.

In Katy Darby's Victorian novel, *The Whore's Asylum*, it is described as being 'the sole vaguely reputable tavern in Jericho'. The area is portrayed as a maze of seedy streets and badly-lit taverns, frequented by prostitutes and drunkards. Katy Darby studied English literature at Somerville College.

Related locations include Jericho, North Oxford and Old Bookbinders Ale House.

Literary Links: Katy Darby

▼ ***The Harcourt Arms.*** (Martin Addison, Wikimedia Commons/Creative Commons)

HEADINGTON

Located on the eastern side of Oxford at the top of a hill, Headington was home to both Tolkien and C.S. Lewis (Tolkien lived at 76 Sandfield Road from 1953 to 1968, Lewis at The Kilns and Joy Davidman at 10 Old High Street). People have been living in the area since the Stone Age but it experienced its greatest growth during the early twentieth century. New housing surrounding the medieval village known as Old Headington created suburbs like Highfield and Quarry. One of its most famous modern landmarks is the Headington Shark sculpture, which sticks out of the roof of a Victorian terraced house. Made by sculptor John Buckley in 1986, it was commissioned by a local radio presenter, Bill Heine.

The many other literary residents of Headington include poet Elizabeth Jennings and science fiction writer Brian Aldiss. Related locations are the Ampleforth Arms, Holy Trinity Church, The Kilns, 10 Old High street, C.S. Lewis Nature Reserve, Sandfield Road and St Andrew's Church.

Literary Links: Brian Aldiss, C.S. Lewis, J.R.R. Tolkien

▼ ***Plaque on 10 Old High Street Headington, occupied by Joy Davidman.*** (Wikimedia Commons/Creative Commons)

HOLY TRINITY CHURCH
46 Quarry Road
Headington
Oxford OX3 8NU
www.hthq.uk

Built between 1848 and 1849 using a Gothic-inspired design by Sir George Gilbert Scott, Holy Trinity is the only parish church by this architect in Oxfordshire. It is built of local stone set amid woodland that is full of wildlife. It is this church that C.S. Lewis attended regularly, just ten minutes' walk from his home at The Kilns.

He is said to have turned the door handle loudly as he entered the church every Sunday morning. The priest in charge, Father Ronald Head, became a friend, taking communion to him during his final illness.

Inside the church visitors can see the pew Lewis preferred to use. Located in the north aisle close to a pillar, it gave him a good view of the pulpit. On one occasion when his attention wandered during a sermon, he mentally created the idea and overall outline for *The Screwtape Letters*, which presents advice from an older devil to a younger one on how to corrupt people. Lewis himself preached from that pulpit on several occasions on varying topics, including

▲ ***The grave of C.S. Lewis, Holy Trinity Church.*** (Steve Daniels, Wikimedia Commons/Creative Commons)

miracles. He was often asked to preach at churches around Oxford.

The 'Narnia Window' always attracts attention, located as it is close to Lewis's pew. This is not a traditional stained-glass window, rather a glass window with designs etched into it. Completed in 1991 by artist Sally Scott, the window acts as a memorial to both Lewis and two local children. The window depicts a garden filled with talking animals, a lantern, the great Lion Aslan, Mr Tumnus the faun, the White Witch, the Beavers and the Pevensey children and their magic gifts. There are images from other Narnia books, such as two children on a flying horse, a small girl flying on a talking owl, the castle of Cair Paravel, a bearded dwarf, a unicorn's head and Reepicheep the mouse. The design stresses that all animals have God's grace.

Lewis is buried under a tree in the churchyard. Tolkien was among the mourners on that cold, windy day with flakes of snow in the air. The memorial stone is simple, just as Lewis wanted.

A video tour entitled 'The Church of C.S. Lewis, A Pilgrim's Guide' can be accessed on the church website. Related locations are the Ampleforth Arms, Headington, The Kilns, 10 Old High Street and the C.S. Lewis Nature Reserve.

Literary Links: C.S. Lewis

HOLYWELL CEMETARY
10 St Cross Road
Oxford
OX1 3TU
www.holywellcemetery.com

Holywell Cemetery has been described as one of Oxford's best kept secrets. It was established in 1847, and initially burials were restricted to members of the Church of England. Over 160 university dons are buried there, along with many professional people from Oxford, including Benjamin

▲ ***Grave of Kenneth Grahame, Holywell Cemetery.***
(William M. Connolley, Wikimedia Commons/Creative Commons)

Blackwell, the first city librarian whose bookshop in St Clements was the forerunner of the famous Blackwell's bookshop founded by his son. Kenneth Grahame and his son are buried here, as is Charles Williams, scholar and friend of J.R.R. Tolkien and C.S. Lewis. George Claridge Druce, author of *Flora of Oxfordshire*, is buried here, while nearby is Sir John Stainer, Professor of Music at the University of Oxford and composer of many hymn tunes, anthems and the *Crucifixion* oratorio. A window to his memory can be seen in St Cross Church.

Literary Links: Kenneth Grahame, Walter Pater, Charles Williams

JERICHO

A historic suburb, Jericho is within walking distance of central Oxford. Historically, it was the place where travellers waited if they arrived after the city gates were closed. It became a residential area, close to the Oxford Canal, catering for working-class people. Unfortunately, it was not very healthy because of poor drainage and open sewers, rendering it susceptible to cholera during the 1832 epidemic.

Following improvements in drainage, it became the setting for red-brick Victorian terraces which ultimately provided homes for many Oxford scholars given its proximity to the open grounds of Port Meadow. Philip Pullman described Jericho as being one of the most fascinating places in Oxford due to its 'history on every corner'.

Access to Jericho is via the path beside the Oxford Canal or by walking along Cornmarket and Woodstock Road.

Jericho features in Colin Dexter's Inspector Morse series. His fifth book was entitled *The Dead of Jericho* and was later adapted as the first episode of the *Inspector Morse* series. It focuses on the story of Inspector Morse meeting Anne Scott at a party. Six months later, she is found dead in Jericho. Subsequently, Jericho was used on several occasions for filming scenes for *Morse*, *Lewis* and *Endeavour*.

The area also features in Philip Pullman's *His Dark Materials* trilogy, with scenes set in Jericho especially around St Barnabas Church, Walton Street and Juxon Street.

Related locations are The Harcourt Arms, Jude the Obscure pub, North Oxford and Old Bookbinders Ale House.

Literary Links: Colin Dexter, Thomas Hardy, Philip Pullman, Charles Williams

JUDE THE OBSCURE PUB

54 Walton Street
Jericho
Oxford
OX2 6AE
www.greeneking.co.uk/pubs/oxford

Originally named the 'Prince of Wales' in 1871, the pub changed its name in 1995 so as to pay tribute to local

▲ ***Jude the Obscure* pub, Jericho.** (Fractal Angel, Wikimedia Commons/Creative Commons/geograph.org)

links with Thomas Hardy's novel. Jericho features in *Jude the Obscure* as 'Beersheba'. The central character moves to Oxford (Christminster). One of his scenes is set in St Barnabas Church which was designed by architect Arthur Blomfield, with whom Thomas Hardy worked as an assistant architect.

The pub is now part of the Greene King chain, and is open daily.

Related locations are The Harcourt Arms, North Oxford and Old Bookbinders Ale House.

Literary Links: Thomas Hardy

NORTHMOOR ROAD
Summertown
OX2 6UR

Located in North Oxford, Northmoor Road is a quiet residential street not far from the Dragon School. J.R.R. Tolkien lived in two Northmoor Road houses between 1926 and 1947. While living at No. 20, he wrote *The Hobbit* and the core manuscript of *The Lord of the Rings*. The building is now Grade II listed. Apparently life could be a little lively when the Tolkiens were living in the street as there are tales of Tolkien charging down the road wearing Viking dress and brandishing weapons on his way to parties.

Another famous resident was Austrian quantum physicist Erwin Schrödinger who subsequently wrote

▲ ***Blue plaque marking J.R.R. Tolkien's home on Northmoor Road.*** (Owen Massey McKnight, Wikimedia Commons/Creative Commons/Flickr)

his famous 'Schrödinger's Cat' paper while living there.

When filming John Le Carré's novel *Tinker, Tailor, Soldier, Spy*, Connie's flat was located on Northmoor road, and Smiley is seen walking to it.

Literary Links: John le Carré, J.R.R. Tolkien

NORTH OXFORD
Jericho and Summertown

There is still a distinctly Victorian ambiance to be found in the North Oxford suburbs, dominated as they are by Victorian-style housing and layout. The area roughly covers Jericho and Summertown plus some adjacent streets. Much of the area was originally owned by various Oxford colleges, particularly St John's. It was these college links that resulted in the development of housing in the area, especially large family houses. In 1877, university fellows were first allowed to marry and live outside the colleges. As a result, colleges sought to provide suitable housing nearby.

During the mid twentieth century, there were attempts by the university and colleges to replace these Victorian houses with smaller, more fashionable ones. This resulted in a major protest, with Sir John Betjeman playing a prominent role. He was a passionate supporter of Victorian architecture and campaigned for the maintenance of North Oxford's Victorian buildings, churches and railway stations. His successful campaigning helped ensure that North Oxford retained its Victorian character. One of his poems was entitled 'May Day Song', written about North Oxford and referring to Belbroughton Road and 'Summerfields to Lynams'.

Literary Links: Sir John Betjeman

OLD BOOKBINDERS ALE HOUSE
17–18 Victor Street
Jericho
Oxford
OX2 6BT
www.oldbookbinders.co.uk
www.craftybelle.uk

A Jericho-based family-run pub, the Old Bookbinders featured several times in the filming of *Morse*, *Lewis* and *Endeavour*, usually as a place where the lead characters stop for a drink and a chat to discuss whatever crime they are trying to solve.

The Old Bookbinders was founded in 1869, to cater for the needs of people working at the nearby Oxford University Press. The name is believed to be unique, with no other pubs in Britain using the name Bookbinders. The streets around the pub housed many of the printers employed by Oxford University Press. Between 1806 and 1834, the overall number of printers in the area increased from ten to ninety. Colin Dexter's book *The Dead of Jericho* mentions the pub, referring

▲ ***Old Bookbinders Ale House.*** (Martin Addison, Wikimedia Commons/Creative Commons/Geograph.org.uk)

to 'The Printers Devil' – a name given to printing apprentices who were frequently covered in black ink after cleaning and adjusting the presses.

It is a popular, quirky pub, serving food and drink most days and attracting a wide clientele of locals and students. Well behaved dogs are welcome.

Literary Links: Colin Dexter

10 OLD HIGH STREET
Headington
Oxford
OX3 9HN

A blue plaque can be seen marking the place where, in 1952, C.S. Lewis met Joy Gresham (née Davidman), an American deserted by her husband. Lewis helped her arrange the rental of the property, for herself and her two boys. One of the boys – Douglas Gresham – later wrote 'It was a nice place partly because so many visitors came'. These included many of Oxford's literary luminaries such as Lewis and J.R.R. Tolkien.

Lewis and Joy married in 1956 at Oxford register office. This was a marriage of convenience in order that she could stay in the UK following her divorce from her first husband. She remained living at No. 10 until 1957, when she married Lewis in a religious ceremony at the hospital where she was being treated for cancer.

The house is not open to the public.

Related locations are the Ampleforth Arms Headington, Holy Trinity Church, The Kilns, Old High Street and the C.S. Lewis Nature Reserve.

LITERARY LINK: C.S. Lewis

2 POLSTEAD ROAD
Oxford
OX2 6TN

This was the family home of T.E. Lawrence (Lawrence of Arabia) from the age of eight. A blue plaque on the outside of the building has recorded this for posterity. It was here that Lawrence was acknowledged as the son of Sir Thomas Chapman. Chapman had an affair with Sarah Junner, a governess, which led to the birth of an illegitimate son. Chapman left his wife and went to live with Sarah and his son, eventually adding more siblings to the family. Having spent time in Ireland, Scotland and Jersey, the family moved to Oxford in 1896 using the names Mr and Mrs Lawrence. T.E. Lawrence lived in Polstead Road until 1921, during which time he attended the City of Oxford High School for Boys in George Street,

'Lawrence House', 2 Polstead Road, home of T.E. Lawrence. (Wikimedia Commons)

Oxford and then read history at Jesus College.

The house is a private residence and is not open to the public.

Literary Links: T.E. Lawrence

SANDFIELD ROAD
Headington
Oxford
OX3 7RG

J.R.R. Tolkien moved to Headington in 1953. He and his family lived in a house at 76 Sandfield Road until 1968. An inscribed plaque over the garage door was installed in the 1970s reflecting his life at the house, showing an image of the dragon Smaug from *The Hobbit*, plus The Hill in Hobbiton with Bag End tunnelled into the Hill, as well as a compass bearing dwarf runes at each point. While living at Sandfield Road, all three books in *The Lord of the Rings* trilogy were published: *The Fellowship of the Ring* (1954), *The Two Towers* (1954) and *The Return of the King* (1955).

Over the years, the popularity of *The Lord of the Rings* attracted so much attention from fans that the Tolkiens left Headington and moved to Poole.

After his death in 1973, a requiem mass was said for Tolkien in the church at which he had worshipped for so many years – St Anthony of Padua Church, Headington.

Literary Links: J.R.R. Tolkien

ST ANDREW'S CHURCH
St Andrew's Road
Headington
Oxford OX3 9DL
www.standrewsheadington.co.uk

No one knows exactly when a church was first built on this site, but it is known that the village of Headington was mentioned in a royal deed of King Ethelred in 1004. King Ethelred may well have been christened at this church.

Believed to be the oldest building in Headington, some parts of the existing church date from the twelfth century. There are some Norman features remaining such as part of the chancel, while the oldest of the bells dates from the mid fifteenth century. The tower was not completed until around 1500. Repairs were undertaken in the mid nineteenth century, but it was felt that the church was not big enough to cope with the number of extra houses being built around Headington. This led to the creation of a new aisle and vestry. The ringing chamber was restored in 1967, allowing all six bells to be rehung. The church follows the Catholic tradition in the Church of England.

The main literary connection for St Andrew's is with the sci-fi writer Brian Aldiss. Although Aldiss was an atheist, he counted Father Michael Brewin of St Andrew's as a close friend. He later told the *Guardian* newspaper that 'One of the things I disliked when I came to Headington was that it was a very Christian community. But the vicar is all right. When Margaret was dying, he was round here often. He was a good man with red wine.'

When Aldiss himself died, he asked for his funeral to be held at St Andrew's and there is a memorial to him in the churchyard.

Literary Links: Brian Aldiss

ST CROSS CHURCH
St Cross Road
Oxford
OX1 3TP

A medieval church located close to Holywell Cemetery, the burial site of Kenneth Grahame of *The Wind in the Willows* fame, St Cross church is now primarily used as a historical collections centre for Balliol College. Much of the church building was rebuilt during the Victorian era in Gothic Revival style. Despite its change of use, St Cross has not been deconsecrated and the chancel is still used for occasional services.

The historic collections stored in the church include rare books, medieval manuscripts and literary, scientific and political papers spanning eight centuries and are regarded as part of the national heritage.

The main literary link is Dorothy L. Sayers who referred to the church in her Lord Peter Wimsey story *Gaudy Night*, and in *Busman's Honeymoon*

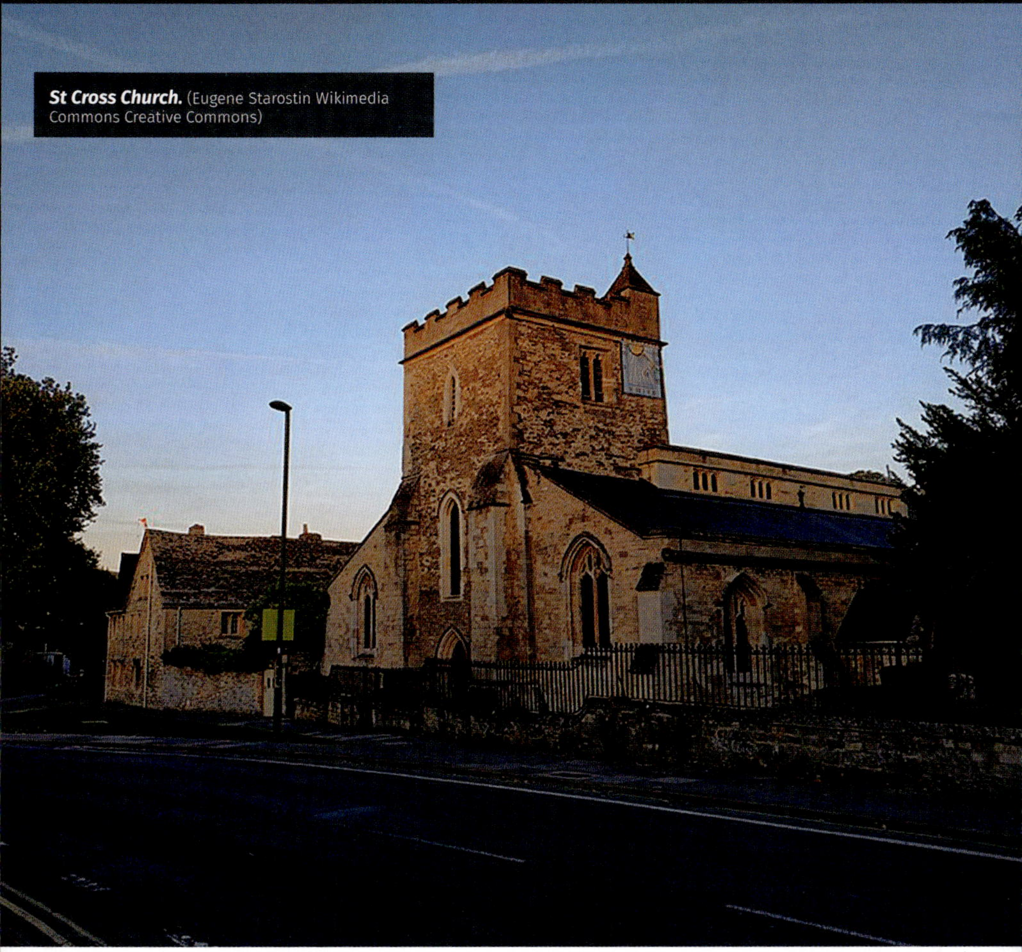

St Cross Church. (Eugene Starostin Wikimedia Commons Creative Commons)

Wimsey marries Harriet Vane at St Cross.

The church is not open to the public.

Literary Links: Dorothy L. Sayers

SUMMERTOWN

A residential area about a mile north of St Giles', most of the houses in Summertown are Victorian, having been built on college land as a result of the decision by the university to allow fellows to marry and have their own homes, rather than being limited to rooms in college.

Numerous writers have lived in this area including Colin Dexter, Dame Iris Murdoch, Desmond Morris and

▲ ***Summertown.*** (Wikimedia Commons Creative Commons)

J.R.R. Tolkien. Colin Dexter worked at the Oxford Examining Board offices in Summertown. The area was frequently used as a film location for the Morse-related TV adaptations.

Literary Links: Colin Dexter, Desmond Morris, Iris Murdoch, J.R.R. Tolkien

THE KILNS

Lewis Close
Headington
Oxford
OX3 8JD
www.cslewis.org

The Kilns was built in 1922 on the site of a former brickworks with a flooded clay pit now forming a lake in the garden. A blue plaque can be seen on the exterior, marking its pivotal role in the story of C.S. Lewis.

Lewis moved into The Kilns in 1930 soon after he had converted to Christianity. Accompanying him were his brother Warnie, Mrs Moore and her daughter Maureen. All of his Christian writing was created here.

The Kilns, located on Lewis Close, is where he wrote the Narnia series. During the Second World War, Lewis offered a home at The Kilns to children being evacuated from the bombing during the London Blitz. It was these children who provided the inspiration for the children in the *Lion,*

▲ ***The Kilns.*** (J. Schroe, Wikimedia Commons/Creative Commons)

the Witch and the Wardrobe. The house was featured in the Narnia stories, along with Lewis's gardener Fred Paxford, who inspired the character of Puddleglum, the Marsh-wiggle who acts as a guide in *The Silver Chair*.

Lewis's wife Joy died at The Kilns in 1960.

The house is not a museum, rather a study centre where scholars can take up residencies or attend seminars. Tours of the house can be arranged by appointment only on Tuesdays, Thursdays and Saturdays.

Related locations are the Ampleforth Arms Headington, Holy Trinity Church and the C.S. Lewis Nature Reserve.

Literary Links: C.S. Lewis

THE TROUT INN
195 Godstow Road
Wolvercote
Oxford
OX2 8PN
www.thetroutoxford.co.uk

This building was constructed in the sixteenth century and by 1625 had been turned into an inn. In 1757, the two-storey building was rebuilt. Today, The Trout remains a popular meeting place with its own riverside garden. It featured in several episodes of *Inspector Morse*, with Morse and Lewis often enjoying a drink by the river. In 'The Wolvercote Tongue', for example, Morse and Lewis stand on the bridge looking at the pub below them. It is

The Trout Inn, Wolvercote.
(Wikimedia Commons/Creative Commons/geography.org.uk)

seen in the background of scenes where divers recover the Anglo-Saxon Wolvercote Tongue from the river, and in 'Who Killed Harry Field?', Morse takes Helen Field to the pub while discussing her husband's murder.

Poet Robert Southey recalled visiting The Trout when he wrote, in his *Letters from England* in 1808: 'We started soon after six, and went by water, rowing up the main stream of the Isis, between level shores ... We ascended the river about a league to Godstow, where we breakfasted at a little ale-house by the water-side.'

In Volume II of *The Collected Letters of C.S. Lewis*, biographer Walter Hooper writes, 'The Trout Inn, one of Lewis's favourite places, is a few miles outside Oxford on Godstow Road, and faces the Thames ... Its interior is very cosy with flagstone floors, beamed ceilings and log fires. The Inklings went there often in the summer when they could have their drinks outside by the river.' On other occasions Lewis, accompanied by Dr Havard and James Dundas-Grant would visit The Trout after a meeting. They would sit on the wall with the Isis flowing beneath them, eating cheese and French bread. A large lion guards the footbridge from the pub to the island.

Sir John Betjeman refers to the Trout in *An Oxford University Chest* (1938), while in Evelyn Waugh's *Brideshead Revisited* we have: 'it's half past five. We'll get to Godstow in time for dinner, drink at The Trout, leave Hardcastle's motor car and walk back by the river'. Dylan Thomas was another frequent visitor during his stay in Oxford.

In Pullman's *His Dark Materials*, The Trout Inn is mentioned as being one of the places to which the nuns supply fruit and vegetables. The Trout used the apples from its orchard to make desserts.

Nearby locations are Wolvercote and the Wolvercote Cemetery.

Literary Links: Sir John Betjeman, Colin Dexter, C.S. Lewis, Robert Southey, Evelyn Waugh, Philip Pullman, Dylan Thomas

THE VICTORIA ARMS PUB
Mill Lane
Marston
Oxford
OX3 0PZ
www.butcombe.com/the-victoria-arms-oxfordshire

This picturesque building dates back to the seventeenth century when it was a ferryman's cottage and apparently at one point hosted Oliver Cromwell.

Overlooking the River Cherwell at Old Marston, just outside central Oxford, The Victoria Arms was used as a filming location for the *Morse*, *Lewis* and *Endeavour* series. On one occasion, Morse is seen reciting part of the A.E. Houseman poem 'How Clear, How Lovely Bright'. A line from the poem

The Victoria Arms seen from the River Cherwell.
(Christopher Whalen, Wikipedia commons/Creative Commons)

was used for the episode's title, 'The Remorseful Day'.

Owned by the Oxford Preservation Trust, The Victoria Arms was almost derelict when purchased in 1959 and under threat of development. Following several years of being operated as a free house, it underwent renovation and was finally reopened in 1986. It is now a popular destination for locals and tourists alike.

The pub is open daily and food is available. Mooring is available for punts.

Literary Links: Colin Dexter

WOLVERCOTE

Oxfordshire

Located approximately three miles north of Oxford, Wolvercote's common adjoins the top part of Port Meadow. Although there has been a settlement here since Anglo-Saxon times, the name Wolvercote had become common usage by the late twelfth century. Links with Oxford date back to the eighteenth century when Oxford University Press was supplied with paper produced at a paper mill in Lower Wolvercote.

Wolvercote featured in the Inspector Morse books by Colin Dexter. An American tourist is found dead in a hotel room. She had been planning to return an ancient artefact, the Wolvercote Tongue, part of a belt buckle, to a museum. A prequel story, 'Trove', also features the Wolvercote Tongue and other Anglo-Saxon artefacts. In Philip Pullman's *His Dark Materials*, Wolvercote was a village in Lyra's world. Evelyn Waugh lived in Wolvercote, and the fictional estate of Brideshead is believed to be partly based on Wolvercote Park.

Nearby locations are The Trout Inn and Wolvercote Cemetery.

Literary Links: Colin Dexter, Philip Pullman

WOLVERCOTE CEMETERY

Banbury Road
Wolvercote
Oxford
OX2 8EE

Tolkien and his wife Edith are both buried in Wolvercote Cemetery, rather

▲ ***Tolkien's grave at Wolvercote Cemetery.***
(Wikimedia Commons/Creative Commons/Twooars)

than in the churchyard attached to the parish church. Sited on land between the Banbury Road and Woodstock Road, the cemetery also contains the grave of Sir Thomas Chapman, father of T.E. Lawrence.

Tolkien's grave is frequently visited by fans, many of whom leave flowers. Apart from their names, the gravestone bears the names of Beren and Lúthien which Tolkien used to describe his relationship with Edith. Not far away is the grave of their eldest son, John.

Literary Links: J.R.R. Tolkien

OXFORDSHIRE

ASTHALL MANOR
Swinbrook
Oxfordshire
OX18 4HW
www.asthallmanor.com

Asthall Manor is a historic house which underwent alterations during the nineteenth century, and again in the early twentieth century after being purchased by Lord Redesdale, father of the Mitford sisters. The family moved into Asthall Manor in 1919. In order to make it a suitable home for his large

Asthall Manor garden. (Asthall Manor)

family, Lord Redesdale added cloisters and converted a barn into a ballroom/ library plus rooms above it, linking to the central house. Writing in *A Life of Contrasts*, Diana Mitford recalled, 'This large room, furnished with hundreds of old books, a grand piano and sofas, with high windows looking south and east, was all the world to my brother and me at Asthall. He played all day, Bach, Mozart, Brahms, and I lay on a sofa, reading and listening.'

The family stayed at Asthall until 1926 when they moved to a modern house Lord Redesdale had built at South Lawn, Swinbrook. According to reports, the new house was not liked, but it does still retain reminders of the girls' varying political views. In *Hons and Rebels*, Jessica Mitford noted there were 'swastikas carved into the glass with a diamond ring, and for every swastika a carefully delineated hammer and sickle'. In later years, Nancy Mitford used her memories of Asthall as inspiration for her fictional Alconleigh.

A private home, Asthall and its walled garden are occasionally open to the

▲ **In the Footsteps of the Mitfords.** (Asthall Manor)

public, usually for workshops and other events such as the theatrical production *In the Footsteps of the Mitfords*.

Literary Links: The Mitford sisters

BINSEY: CHURCH OF ST MARGARET OF ANTIOCH
Binsey Lane
Oxford
OX2 0NG

Dating from the twelfth century, the Church of St Margaret of Antioch at Binsey is located on the site of a monastery dedicated to St Frideswide, the patron saint of Oxford. According to the stories, St Frideswide sought sanctuary in Binsey in order to avoid marrying a Mercian prince named Agar. While searching for her, Prince Agar was blinded by lightning. Frideswide prayed for him and a healing spring emerged. By washing his eyes in the water, he regained his sight. The healing properties of the well caused many pilgrims to visit it during the medieval period, and it is said the church was adorned with the crutches of people who had been healed. The well was restored in 1874 when the Rev. T.J. Prout brought it back into use.

Lewis Carroll turned St Margaret's Well into a 'treacle well' in *Alice in*

▼ ***St Margaret of Antioch and her Well*** (© Osney Benefice Office, St Peter and St Paul)

Wonderland, reflecting the fact that treacle referred to a healing fluid in medieval England. The Dormouse tells a story about three sisters who lived at the bottom of the well.

'Well services' are still held during the summer, during which the congregation is sprinkled with the water.

The well sits within the grounds of the medieval Church of St Margaret. Much of the church was rebuilt in the thirteenth century, and the stained glass windows include medieval glass images of St Thomas á Becket and St Margaret of Antioch.

The churchyard offers evidence of other links to the *Alice in Wonderland* story. Memorials to many generations of the Prickett family can be seen. This family lived in the farmhouse just beyond the churchyard and one of the Pricketts was Alice Liddell's governess.

During his stay in Oxford, Dylan Thomas was a frequent visitor to The Perch at Binsey.

Literary Links: Lewis Carroll, Dylan Thomas

BLENHEIM PALACE
Woodstock
OX20 1PS
www.bleinheimpalace.com

One of the largest historic houses in the UK, Blenheim started as a reward for John Churchill, Duke of Marlborough, for his military triumphs during the War of the Spanish Succession which culminated in the Battle of Blenheim in 1704. Designed in the English baroque style by Vanbrugh, it is surrounded by extensive grounds and is the home of the Churchill family. By far the most well-known member of the family is Winston, wartime leader during the Second World War.

The site covers the former Palace of Woodstock, which acted as a royal hunting preserve. During the medieval

'Blenheim Palace, gardens and estate. (Blenheim Palace Park and Gardens)

period, Henry II housed his mistress Rosamund Clifford in what was described as a 'bower and labyrinth'. A spring named after her still exists on the site.

Visitors can explore the extensive grounds, as well as visiting the state rooms and the Churchill exhibition. Extra tours are available focusing on the private apartments, secret corridors and the life of palace staff during a 'downstairs' tour. There is an entry charge.

Blenheim Palace has appeared in numerous books, for example *Death at Blenheim Palace* by Robin Paige and *The Fallen Woman* by Fiona McIntosh. In Jane Austen's *Pride and Prejudice*, Blenheim gets a mention when Lizzie is about to set off for Derbyshire with her aunt and uncle. There are many non-fiction books focusing on the story of Blenheim Palace and Winston Churchill, such as Lady Henrietta Spencer-Churchill's *Blenheim: 300 Years of Life in a*

Palace, Margaret Forster's *Churchill's Grandmama* and Andrew Kearney's *Percy at the Palace*.

One of the most famous literary links is Blenheim's involvement with Harry Potter. Down on the lakeside, a massive cedar of Lebanon has gained the name of the 'Harry Potter Tree'. It was used in the filming of the 2007 film *Harry Potter and the Order of the Phoenix* in the scene in which Professor Snape recalls an episode when, as a student at Hogwarts, he was bullied by Harry Potter's father while sitting under the tree.

The cedar of Lebanon is one of the oldest trees in the grounds, having been planted during Lancelot

▲ ***Filming at the 'Harry Potter Tree'.*** (Blenheim Palace)

▼ ***The 'Harry Potter Tree'.*** (Blenheim Palace)

Capability Brown's eighteenth-century creation of the landscaped gardens.

Literary Links: Jane Austen, J.K. Rowling, Winston Churchill

BLEWBURY
Didcot
Oxfordshire
www.blewbury.co.uk

A pretty village complete with thatched cottages fourteen miles south of Oxford, Blewbury has history dating back centuries. There is an Iron Age fort on Blewburton Hill, while a Saxon charter of 944 refers to 'Bleobyrig' as

Boham's House, home to Kenneth Grahame between 1910 and 1920. (Wikimedia Commons/Creative Commons)

being a 'venerable' village'. During the twentieth century, Blewbury was home to numerous artists and authors such as painter John Revell and authors Kenneth Grahame and Marguerite Steen. Kenneth Grahame lived at Boham's House in Westbrook Street between 1910 and 1920. A blue plaque can be seen on the house marking his presence.

Literary Links: Kenneth Grahame

CHARLBURY
Oxfordshire
OX7 3HH
www.charlbury.info

Located in the Evenlode Valley, Charlbury is a picturesque Oxfordshire town close to Wychwood Forest. Dating back to Anglo-Saxon times, Charlbury includes historic houses such as Cornbury Park, a seventeenth-century country house. Crime writer Veronica Stallwood made Charlbury her home, and wrote numerous novels relating to Oxford.

LITERARY LINK: Veronica Stallwood

EWELME: ST MARY THE VIRGIN
Parson's Green
Ewelme
Oxfordshire
OX10 6PH
www.friendsofewelmechurch.co.uk

Possessing a black and white chequerboard-style frontage complete with battlements, St Mary the Virgin at Ewelme is extremely distinctive. The church owes much of its design to the Chaucer family. Geoffrey Chaucer's son,

▼ ***St Mary the Virgin church, Ewelme.*** (© Oswald Bertram, Wikimedia Commons)

Thomas, obtained the manor of Ewelme as a result of his marriage to Matilda. Their daughter Alice married the Duke of Suffolk. In 1437, Thomas and Alice Chaucer set up the Ewelme Trust with a royal licence from Henry VI to found a church on the site. The trust still exists.

A helm bearing the Chaucer crest can be seen in the church. The alabaster tomb of Alice de la Pole (née Chaucer) bears an effigy of the duchess wearing her coronet and the Order of the Garter wrapped around her left forearm. Underneath the image is another portrait of Alice, showing her in her shroud.

Literary Links: Geoffrey Chaucer

FINSTOCK
Oxfordshire

Finstock is a small village about two miles south of Charlbury and fifteen miles north west of Oxford. People have been living in this area since Roman times, but the first written accounts can be found in the Domesday Book of 1086 when it formed part of land belonging to the Bishop of Lincoln. In 1135, the village was referred to as Fynstoke. The name means 'woodpecker place'. It has several links with Oxford. Sir Thomas White, founder of St John's College, owned the land and it eventually became part of the college's endowment. John Wesley stayed

Approaching Finstock. (Vieve Forward, Wikimedia Commons/Creative Commons)

at Finstock Manor during a preaching visit to the area, T.S. Eliot was received into the Church of England at Finstock's Holy Trinity Church, and novelist Barbara Pym lived at Barn Cottage, Finstock, and is buried in the churchyard.

Literary Links: T.S. Eliot, Barbara Pym, John Wesley

FLEECE PUB, WITNEY

Dylan Thomas broadcast an episode of *Country Magazine* for the BBC Home Service on 8 February 1948 from The Fleece, while he was living in South Leigh.

Literary Links: Dylan Thomas

FOUR SHIRE STONE

Moreton-in-Marsh
Gloucestershire
GL56 0LJ
www.fourshirestone.org.uk

While not strictly in Oxfordshire, being located just outside the village of Moreton-in-Marsh on the A44, the stone marks the point where four counties met: Oxfordshire, Gloucestershire, Warwickshire and Worcestershire. Following the redrawing of county boundaries in 1931, only three counties now meet at this spot: Oxfordshire, Gloucestershire and Warwickshire. Made from blocks of locally quarried honey-coloured Cotswold stone, it is topped with a dome, cornice, ball and finial taking the monument to over 3 metres in height. Local records indicate that the monument stands on the site of a much earlier Four Shire Stone with written references going back to the sixteenth century. A survey of Worcestershire written in the sixteenth century refers to a stone which touches on four shires at this particular point.

Tolkien visited the area on many occasions as it was roughly halfway between Oxford, where he lived, and Evesham, where his brother owned a farm. The Bell Inn at Moreton-in-Marsh was where they met, and it is believed to be the inspiration for the Prancing Pony at Bree. The Four Shire Stone became the Three Farthing Stone in the Shire, marking the meeting place of the Westfarthing, Southfarthing and Eastfarthing.

Literary Links: J.R.R. Tolkien

GODSTOW

Oxfordshire

Godstow is a popular haunt with fans of *Alice in Wonderland*, since it was during that summer afternoon boating trip to Godstow and a picnic by the river that Lewis Carroll began creating the story of a little girl falling down a rabbit hole into Wonderland. He began the story with the words, 'Alice was beginning to get very tired of sitting by her sister on the bank and having nothing to do.'

Just over two miles outside Oxford, Godstow is a pretty location complete with a weir, a bridge over the Thames and a pub linked to Colin Dexter's Morse novels. A short distance upstream is the town of Wolvercote. One of the most noticeable features at Godstow are the ruins of Godstow Abbey, sometimes referred to as Godstow Nunnery. During medieval times, it was occupied by Benedictine nuns and was the home of Fair Rosamund (Rosamund Clifford, the mistress of Henry II). Her grave is somewhere within the grounds.

Philip Pullman used the ruins as a setting for a nunnery dedicated to St Rosamund in the *His Dark Materials* universe. As a young child, Lyra Belacqua stayed here for a few weeks before moving to Jordan College. In the book, Pullman describes her bedroom as initially dark until the nuns changed the wallpaper to cream and added some rugs to the floor. During a flood, many of the nuns died and the building was left in ruins.

Literary Links: Lewis Carroll, Colin Dexter, Philip Pullman

Godstow Lock, looking towards Port Meadow.
(Wikimedia Commons/Creative Commons/AstacopsisGouldi)

ISLIP
Kidlington
Oxfordshire

Islip is a village on the River Ray, five miles north of Oxford. It is said that Edward the Confessor was born in Islip and was baptised in the church. His death in 1066 led to the Norman invasion and the arrival of William the Conqueror, whose Domesday Book recorded a settlement at Islip. The village is sited close to the River Cherwell.

Robert Graves lived in Islip between 1921 and 1926. He described his life in the village in *Goodbye to All That*. There is a blue plaque marking his links with the village on the house in Collice Street that he shared with Nancy Nicholson.

LITERARY LINK: Robert Graves

KELMSCOTT MANOR
Kelmscott
Lechlade
GL7 3HJ
www.kelmscottmanor.org.uk

Built around 1600, the manor was leased by William Morris in 1871. He had been looking for house in a rural area, so as to get his family away from

▼ ***Aerial View of Islip.*** (Dave Price, Wikipedia Commons/Creative Commons)

the unhealthy London environment. The Morris family initially rented it with Dante Gabriel Rossetti, the Pre-Raphaelite artist, but Rossetti only stayed until 1874. For William Morris, Kelmscott was his perfect home, which he described as being 'heaven on earth'. Although he was never able to spend as much time as he had hoped at Kelmscott, it was his preferred home and provided continual inspiration both for designs such as Strawberry Thief and writing like *News from Nowhere*. It was here that he founded the Kelmscott Press and where his fantasy novel *The Wood Beyond the World* was written. This novel is extremely important in the fantasy genre since it was the first to combine an imaginary world with the supernatural, leading to modern-day fantasy literature. It inspired C.S. Lewis to develop the idea of a wood between worlds which he then combined with the concept of a well taken from another of William Morris's novels, *The Well at the World's End*. The combination of these two elements helped develop the idea of the 'Wood between the Worlds' used in *The Magician's Nephew* and also referred to in *The Last Battle*.

After the death of William Morris, the trustees of his estate acquired Kelmscott for his wife, and it later

▼ ***Kelmscott Manor.*** (Wikimedia Commons Creative Commons)

passed to his younger daughter. The long-term aim was to provide a facility for artists and scholars. Although Kelmscott was controlled by the University of Oxford for some years, it was eventually taken over by the Society of Antiquaries of London who undertook a major restoration project.

Kelmscott is now preserved as it was when William Morris and his family lived there. There are special exhibitions and educational activities complementing general visits. The house and grounds are open during the main season from April to the end of October. There is an entry charge to the house. Entry to the gardens and grounds is free. There is a tea room and shop on site.

LITERARY LINK: William Morris

NETTLEBED
Oxfordshire

A small village in the Chilterns, Nettlebed is just six miles from Wallingford. The village dates back to medieval times, and is on an ancient route between London and Oxford. It was the childhood home of writer Ian Fleming. Nettlebed has been used as a filming location for episodes of *Midsomer Murders* including 'The Maid in Splendour', 'Dance with the Dead', 'The Magician's Nephew' and 'The Ballad of Midsomer County'.

LITERARY LINK: Ian Fleming

ROLLRIGHT STONES
Rollright Road
Little Rollright
Chipping Norton
Oxfordshire
OX7 5QB
www.rollrightstones.co.uk

An atmospheric prehistoric site on the borders of Oxfordshire and Warwickshire, the Rollright Stones includes the 4,000-year-old stone circle

known as the King's Men, together with the Whispering Knights, an even older 'portal dolmen' burial chamber. Also present on the site is the King Stone believed to date from around 1,500 BCE. All the stones are made of Jurassic limestone sourced from the Cotswold hills. The stones are mentioned in the twelfth-century *Wonders of Britain*. There are many legends about the stones, including a tale about how they were once a king and his knights who were turned to stone by a witch. They return temporarily to life on certain saints days or when the church clock strikes midnight. J.R.R. Tolkien explored countless ancient remains around Oxford, and many observers have since suggested that the Rollright Stones may have been the inspiration for the Barrow Downs, on which the hobbits are ensnared by a malevolent barrow-wight.

Literary Links: J.R.R. Tolkien

Rollright Stones. (Simon Burchell, Wikimedia Commons)

SOUTH LEIGH
South Leigh & High Cogges
Oxfordshire

South Leigh is a small rural village in West Oxfordshire, and the first mention of the village was recorded in 1190. It's most notable literary resident was poet Dylan Thomas who lived there between September 1947 and May 1949 together with his wife Caitlin and their young daughter. They lived in an old farmhouse known as South Leigh Manor. He recalled the site flooding in winter, while in summer the long grass had to be cut by his wife using a scythe while hoping that there were no children hiding in the grass. They spent many evenings at the Mason Arms public house in the village. Caitlin was known to dance among the tables, while Dylan played shove ha'penny. He was working on *Under Milk Wood* at the time, and some of the local people later told journalists that some villagers people had inspired the characters of No Good Boyo and Mrs Dai Bread.

Literary Links: Dylan Thomas

SWINBROOK: ST MARY'S CHURCH
Swinbrook
Oxfordshire
OX18 4DY
www.swinbrookat11.org

A small twelfth-century church, St Mary's is now linked as a parish to St John the Baptist church in nearby Burford. Most of the church was designed in Romanesque and early Gothic style while the tower was added

▼ ***South Leigh village.*** (Chris Brown, Wikimedia Commons/Creative Commons/geograph.org.uk)

▲ ***Graves of Nancy, Unity and Diana Mitford at St Mary's churchyard, Swinbrook.*** (Wikimedia Commons/geograph.org)

in 1822. One of the most stunning features are the highly decorative carved wooden misericords bearing images such as a dragon and a woman with her hands on her knees, which are located alongside the south wall of the chancel. In 2010, Deborah Mitford recalled licking the pews while kneeling for prayers.

Fou of the Mitford sisters, Nancy, Unity, Diana and Pamela, together with their parents, are buried in St Mary's Churchyard. Inside the church, a memorial plaque to their brother Tom can be seen. The Mitford family lived at Swinbrook House.

The church featured in the filming of Helen Fielding's novel *Bridget Jones's Diary*, as the location where Bridget's newborn child was baptised.

Literary Links: Helen Fielding, the Mitford sisters

SWINBROOK: THE SWAN INN
Swinbrook
Oxfordshire
OX18 4DY
www.theswanswinbrook.co.uk

Once owned by Deborah Mitford, Duchess of Devonshire, this pretty inn is located on the banks of the River Windrush. There are pictures of all the Mitford sisters on the walls of the restaurant.

Deborah grew up in Swinbrook and retained an affection for the area until her death. In 2010, the duchess attended a 'Wait for Me' book signing at the Swan Inn during which she said, 'Asthall followed by Swinbrook have been such a part of a my life that I still feel it's home here.' The Swan has also been the setting for filming scenes from *Downtown Abbey*, for example when Lady Sybil eloped with the chauffeur.

The Swan Inn is open daily for food and drink. Accommodation is also available.

Literary Links: The Mitford sisters

UFFINGTON
Oxfordshire
www.nationaltrust.org.uk/whitehorsehill

The White Horse of Uffington is one of the most well-known sites in Oxfordshire. Dating back to prehistoric times, the giant horse figure measures 110 metres long and is created from deep trenches cut into the chalk hill. Now owned and managed by the National Trust, it is regularly scoured (cleaned) to ensure it maintains its pristine colour.

This giant horse has inspired many authors over the years. Thomas Hughes, author of *Tom Brown's Schooldays*, was born in Uffington and wrote a book entitled *The Scouring of the White Horse*, while G.K. Chesterton features the scouring of the White Horse in his poem 'The Ballad of the White Horse'. Children's author Rosemary Sutcliffe wrote *Sun Horse, Moon Horse* about the creator of the horse, and Charles Todd used the horse as a feature in his detective novel *A Pale Horse*. There have been suggestions that the horse inspired the banner flown by the horsemen of Rohan in J.R.R. Tolkien's Middle Earth since the White Horse would have been very familiar to Tolkien.

In the village of Uffington itself, the medieval Great Coxwell Barn was well known to William Morris and his family. Morris wrote that the barn, a relic of a monastic grange, was 'unapproachable in its dignity, as beautiful as a cathedral, yet with no ostentation of the builder's art'. In 1996 the Society for the Protection of Ancient Buildings (SPAB), founded by Morris, engraved the name of Morris and his dates on the barn door. This was to mark the hundredth anniversary of Morris's death.

John Betjeman lived at Garrards Farmhouse, where visitors included Evelyn Waugh. He wrote *Summoned by Bells* while living in Uffington.

Literary Links: John Betjeman, G.K. Chesterton, Thomas Hughes, William Morris, Rosemary Sutcliffe, Charles Todd, J.R.R. Tolkien

WALLINGFORD
Oxfordshire
OX10 8DL
www.wallingfordtowncouncil.gov.uk

Located on the banks of the River Thames, there has been a settlement here since the Bronze Age. It was one of King Alfred's fortified towns designed to protect against Viking assaults. The castle originates from this period, and was later expanded and strengthened under the Normans. Poet Geoffrey Chaucer's son Thomas was appointed constable of the castle in 1399. In the *Midsomer Murders* series, Wallingford is turned into Causton and its police station features in the books by Caroline Graham. Dylan Thomas was a frequent visitor to the George Hotel while staying with his friends Margaret and A.J.P. Taylor in Oxford.

▲ ***Agatha Christie statue, Wallingford.***
(Wallingford Town Council)

By far its most well known citizen was crime writer Agatha Christie. The town's narrow streets and marketplace would have been very familiar to her since she lived close by at Winterbrook. She was frequently seen around the town visiting the shops, and was president of the Sinodun Players, a local drama society.

She used the name Wallingford in her book *Cards on the Table*. The town is also believed to be the origin of the description she gives of the fictional town of Market Basing in *Dumb Witness*: 'It had an air of old fashioned dignity and quietude about it. Its one wide street and ample market square seemed to say, "I was a place of importance once and to any person of sense and breeding I am still the same ... I was built to endure in a day when solidarity and beauty went hand in hand."'

Wallingford holds an annual festival devoted to Agatha Christie every September. A five-mile Agatha Christie Trail can be downloaded at www.wallingfordtowncouncil.gov.uk/visitors/agatha-christie. The trail is designed to take visitors around all the places linked to Agatha Christie and her life in Wallingford and the nearby hamlet of Winterbrook. Typical locations include the Kinecroft, where a life-size bronze statue of Agatha Christie can be seen sitting on a bench, and the meadows in which Agatha used to walk.

The Wallingford Museum houses a permanent Agatha Christie exhibition including some of her original letters as well as a collection of local stories from people who knew her in the area.

When travelling by rail, Agatha Christie and Max Mallowan used the branch line from Wallingford to Cholsey in order to connect with main line services to Oxford and London. Today, this branch line is operated by the heritage Cholsey & Wallingford Railway which uses steam and diesel locomotives pulling coaches dating from the 1950s. The line passes the churchyard at Cholsey in which Agatha and Max are buried. A round trip takes approximately three-quarters of an hour.

In honour of Agatha Christie, the Cholsey & Wallingford Railway periodically operates murder mystery events with a 1930s/1940s theme. Participants question suspects and try to solve the murder.

Literary Links: Geoffrey Chaucer, Agatha Christie, Caroline Graham, Dylan Thomas

WANTAGE
Oxfordshire

Historically part of Berkshire, Wantage was transferred to Oxfordshire as a result of local authority changes in 1974. The birthplace of King Alfred the Great in 849, the town has a long history dating back to Roman times. It also has links with pantomime story Dick Whittington, since Alice FitzWarin, wife of Dick Whittington, three times mayor of London, grew up in Wantage. Visitors can even see her father's memorial in the church.

More recently, Wantage was the home of poet laureate John Betjeman. He lived at The Mead between 1951 and 1972, and his wife owned King Alfred's teashop in the centre of town. The teashop's slogan was 'Burnt cakes a speciality', and it was a popular meeting place for both locals and car-owning undergraduate students. During this time, Betjeman wrote many of his most famous poems such as 'A Subaltern's Love Song', 'Wantage Bells' and 'On Leaving Wantage'. He was a familiar sight strolling along the Letcombe Brook footpath to visit the vicarage. Betjeman was a church warden at the Church of St Peter and St Paul.

The Betjeman Millenium Park occupies a two-acre plot of land between the parish church, Letcombe Brook and Leat Stream. It is an area that would have been extremely familiar to John Betjeman, since his home was just above the park. Apart from its pleasant natural environment, it has a poetry trail comprising plaques linked to Betjeman. Discovery is seen as a key theme of the trail, with visitors encouraged to follow extracts from his poems as they flow from stone to stone.

▲ ***John Betjeman outside the Vale and Downland Museum*** (Vale & Downland Museum)

A bust of Betjeman can be seen in the Vale and Downland Museum, situated in the centre of town. In addition to the links to Betjeman, the museum contains numerous displays exploring the area's cultural history.

Literary Links: Sir John Betjeman

WINTERBROOK
Wallingford
OX10 9SL

Located just thirteen miles south of Oxford on the banks of the River Thames close to the town of Wallingford, the little hamlet of Winterbrook is believed to have inspired the creation of the village of St Mary Mead from Agatha Christie's Miss Marple novels and stories.

Agatha Christie knew this village well. In 1934, she and her husband, archaeologist Max Mallowan, purchased Winterbrook House. This became their home for the rest of their lives, with Agatha dying there in 1976. There is now a blue plaque commemorating her life at Winterbrook House.

▲ ***Agatha Christie and Max Mallowan in 1950.*** (Wikimedia National Portrait Gallery)

A Grade II eighteenth-century listed building, Winterbrook House is not open to the public.

While living at Winterbrook House, Agatha Christie and Max Mallowan regularly attended services at the nearby church of St Mary, Cholsey. Both Agatha and Max are buried in a corner of St Mary's churchyard, overlooking the countryside. Close to St Mary's Church is a road sign marked 'St Mary Mead', which is believed to have inspired the name used in the Miss Marple stories.

Literary Links: Agatha Christie

WOODSTOCK
Oxfordshire

A small market town located adjacent to Blenheim Palace, Woodstock was featured in Colin Dexter's Inspector Morse novel, *Last Bus to Woodstock*. Chaucer's House in Woodstock was once the home of Thomas Chaucer, son of the poet Geoffrey Chaucer.

Over the centuries, Woodstock has been home to royalty. Henry II courted his mistress Rosamund Clifford (Fair Rosamund) at Woodstock. Edward the Black Prince, eldest son of King Edward III, was born at Woodstock Manor, while in the reign of Queen Mary I, Elizabeth Tudor (later Elizabeth I) was imprisoned at Woodstock. During her imprisonment, Elizabeth wrote 'Much suspected by me, None proved can be.' Winston Churchill is buried at the nearby village of Bladen.

Woodstock was the venue for a meeting between John Le Carré and MI5's George Leggett, during which Le Carré was persuaded to continue working for British Intelligence while an undergraduate at Oxford University. He was required to 'adopt a left-wing persona' and spy on communist activities among fellow students.

Literary Links: Colin Dexter, John le Carré

Woodstock. (P.L. Chadwick, Wikimedia Commons/Creative Commons)